To Jack
with love from
Dad

Sept. 9 - 1933

JEWELS OF ROMANCE & RENOWN

T. WERNER LAURIE LIMITED
24 & 26 Water Lane, London, E.C.4.

(*Bassano*).

QUEEN MARY WEARING THE DIAMOND HEAD-DRESS THAT HAS THE
KOH-I-NOOR IN THE CENTRE.

JEWELS
OF
ROMANCE
AND
RENOWN

By
MARY ABBOTT

Illustrated

LONDON
T. WERNER LAURIE LTD
24 & 26 WATER LANE, E.C.4

THIS VOLUME WAS FIRST PUB-
LISHED IN MCMXXXIII. PRINTED
IN GREAT BRITAIN AT THE ALCUIN
PRESS, CAMPDEN, GLOS. COPY-
RIGHT & ALL RIGHTS RESERVED

TO MY FRIEND
GLADYS DAVIDSON
WHOSE IDEA THIS BOOK WAS
AND WHOSE ENCOURAGEMENT
SPURRED ME TO MAKE IT

ACKNOWLEDGMENTS

MY THANKS are due to Sir Charles Starmer and to the Editors of the Starmer Group of morning and evening newspapers for permission to use portions of articles that I have contributed to the *Birmingham Gazette*, *Evening Despatch* (Birmingham), *Northern Echo* (Darlington), *Nottingham Journal*, *Oxford Mail*, and *Yorkshire Observer* (Bradford).

For a like privilege I also thank the editors of the *Daily Mail*, *Daily Independent* (Sheffield) and the *Queen*.

I also gratefully acknowledge my indebtedness to the Adjutant to H.R.H. the Crown Prince of Norway, to the Consul-General for Norway in London, and to the Consul-General for Sweden in London, each of whom very kindly furnished me with information about royal jewels that I could not otherwise have possessed.

My gratitude is also offered to Miss Ernestine Manton for the very great help she gave me towards the chapter on 'Beauteous Boxes.'

MARY ABBOTT

CONTENTS

ILLUSTRATIONS

Chapter I
DIAMONDS OF DESTINY

MINUS the eight arches of Imperial significance and its cap of purple velvet rimmed with heraldic miniver, the all-diamond crown made for Queen Mary to be crowned with by King George at the Coronation in 1911, is usually the head-dress her Majesty wears at the first Court of the London season. And when that is so, those privileged to pass the presence, glimpse one of the most famous diamonds in the world, the historic Koh-i-Nor. For there it gleams, a 'Mountain of Light' in a Maltese cross setting, flanked by diamond fleurs-de-lis above a circlet, all York roses and small square crosses in diamonds, resting on the Queen's prettily greying hair.

Why the Koh-i-Nor should adorn the Queen-consort's and not the king-regnant's crown, makes an interesting bit of jewel history. When it was given to Queen Victoria by the British East India Company on the annexation of the Punjab in 1850, a hint was dropped that India as a whole would be best pleased if her Britannic Majesty wore the jewel purely as a personal ornament and did not make it part of the British Crown Regalia. So gradually there grew up the belief that should the Koh-i-Nor ever be worn by a man-ruler of Great Britain, India would be lost to the British Empire. And that is why Queen Victoria speci-

1

fically bequeathed this jewel not to her successor on the throne, King Edward, but to his wife. In doing so she made the Koh-i-Nor a royal heirloom to descend to female entail from one reigning monarch's consort to the next. Hence its appearance in Queen Alexandra's coronation diadem and then in Queen Mary's.

In Persia is to be found the sister diamond to the Koh-i-Nor, the Darya-i-Nor or 'Sea of Light,' and according to Persian tradition both gems once gleamed in the sword scabbard of the famous Afrasiab who lived three thousand years B.C. But neither is intrinsically as valuable as it was originally, the Koh-i-Nor on account of bad cutting which reduced its first weight from seven hundred carats to one hundred and six carats, the Darya-i-Nor because it is engraved with the name of a Shah. That both gems are beyond price historically has long been generally understood, but Persia has now told the world so definitely, by publishing the official statement to that effect made by the French experts called in to appraise the Persian Crown Jewels.

'Diamonds of Destiny' a famous French diplomat once called the Koh-i-Nor and the Darya-i-Nor. But what of that other huge diamond out of Persia, the one which a bygone Shah surrendered to Russia as an indemnity for the murder of the Russian Ambassador Griboyedov? Or the Orloff diamond, that wonderful yellow stone set atop the

Russian Imperial sceptre? Tradition says that that gem was looted from an idol in a Hindu temple, taken to Persia, and there stolen by a French soldier who concealed it in a self-inflicted wound in the calf of his leg until he was able to get away with it to India. There he sold it to an Armenian trader from whom Prince Orloff bought it for £40,000 in order to present it to the Empress Catherine II. That was in 1772; now the Soviet Government are asking two millions for it.

But for being set in the Imperial sceptre, the Orloff diamond might have stood in need of being duplicated in paste during the reign of Tzar Nicholas I. For that monarch's German-born wife was so erratic and so fond of jewels that once, when she was about to start on a visit to a little bathing-place in Bavaria famous for the strengthening virtues of its air and water, she suddenly announced her intention of taking all the Crown diamonds with her in addition to the enormous collection of precious gems which were her own private possession. As it was useless trying to thwart her, the Prince who was the State guardian of her Imperial Majesty's person and jewels, got over the difficulty by having a complete facsimile of the Crown jewels made in paste. Petersburg being famous for its jewel-setters and there being no stint of secret service money, the job could be done quickly and without trouble.

This particular empress was so eccentric that

whenever she went to the theatre her dresser had
to bring a bandbox containing a gown and a parure of jewels other than those her Majesty was
wearing, so that if the whim seized the royal lady,
which it fequently did, she could retire to the
room behind the Imperial box and make a complete change of toilette, jewels and all!

To see the third largest diamond in the world—
the Regent—one has only to visit the Louvre in
Paris. And what pictures of the past a glimpse of
that gem conjures up! An eastern slave selling it
for a mere song to a British Governor-General of
Madras in the early eighteenth century. It being
sold again, this time for more than £130,000, the
buyer the French Regent Duke of Orleans. A
costume ball at the palace of Versailles with Queen
Marie Antoinette, garbed as Gabriel d'Estrées,
wearing the 'Regent' to fasten the white ostrich
plumes in her big black hat. A coronation in
Notre-Dame with Napoleon flaunting the diamond in the hilt of his best sword as he crowns
himself emperor and then stoops to crown the
kneeling Josephine, empress.

That was the Regent diamond's last 'great
day.' But it still gathered to itself a morsel more
of romance when it disappeared from the Tuileries Palace during the turmoil that followed Napoleon's adbication, and a year later turned up in a
tavern.

As for the famous blue diamond which used to

share honours with the 'Regent' when there were
kings and queens in France, that was never re-
gained as a national possession after it disappeared
with the rest of the French Regalia in 1792.
Destiny did not intend for it a future of days spent
in the spectacular seclusion of an electric-lit glass-
case at the Louvre, followed by a nightly descent
into the bowels of the earth clamped close with
iron shutters. After thirty years of discreet obscur-
ity the wonderful blue gem was to know nights of
gladness on a woman's bosom, and days of drab-
ness in the covetous atmosphere of world-famous
auction rooms. For, once it had emerged into the
open again and passed from a Paris dealer to an
English collector for the sum of eighteen thousand
pounds sterling, it was to change owners several
times. Change its name, too, though that only
once, when it became known as the Hope diamond
after its first English owner. What the Hope diamond would fetch were it to come into the market
now, nobody can predict, but twenty years ago it
was publicly sold for sixty thousand pounds.

That diamonds which have helped to make
European history should be treasured by eastern
potentates, is turning the tables with a vengeance,
but so it is with several which the Maharajah of
Patiala is immensely proud of. One, known as the
Sancy diamond, was worn as a hat jewel by Charles the Bold Duke of Burgundy before he lost it
during the battle of Nancy. Found by a Swiss

soldier and sold to the French nobleman whose name it bears, the Sancy diamond was subsequently borrowed by Henry III of France to use as a pledge when there was not enough cash in the State coffers to pay for his extravagances.

One hundred years later the Sancy diamond became the property of James II of England, and but for his abdication when he skipped away to France with the gem in his breeches pocket, it might now be among the British Crown Jewels.

Then, of course, it would never have figured among the French Crown Jewels immediately prior to the Revolution, have been lost during that upheaval, and later acquired by a Russian Grand Duke, as its history tells.

Perhaps the Sancy diamond has reached its spiritual home at last. For it is now attached as pendant to that other of the Maharajah of Patiala's much prized possessions out of France—a necklace of diamonds so proudly worn by the Empress Eugénie at the zenith of her power and beauty.

And if the history of the necklace is less hectic than that of the pendant it is not without some purple patches. At the downfall of the Second Empire it was hurriedly bundled in newspaper and thrust into the Princess Metternich's boot-cupboard and thus harboured to safety soon after the Empress Eugénie had fled across the Channel to England and exile.

6

Many other of the French Empress's jewels came that way, too. Indeed, if they had not, she would have fared sparely for the rest of her long life. As it was a goodly sum was realised by the sale of her tiaras, necklaces, bracelets, brooches and earrings, when they were put up for auction at Christie's in 1872. One ring alone, set with a pink diamond surrounded by brilliants, fetched four hundred guineas. But then, it had once belonged to the Empress Josephine, so it was twice blest with Imperial prestige.

Until a few years ago the world's most celebrated jewels were chiefly on this side of the Atlantic. Then the Duke of Westminster sent the Nassac diamond to New York to be sold. Though not as big as the Koh-i-Nor the Nassac is quite as famed in eastern myth and legend, and its romantically lurid past had been thrilling English Court circles for more than a decade when the Koh-i-Nor arrived in London as a gift to Queen Victoria. The first authentic mention of the Nassac diamond dates from the Middle Ages when it served as the eye of the great image of Shiva in the rock temple at Nassac on the Upper Godavery River not far from the original Golconda mine. It was captured by the East India Company's troops in 1818 from an Indian who had plundered the temple, and it was brought to England by Warren Hastings, the first Governor General of India.

But the Nassac diamond never had quite such a

narrow escape of not reaching these shores as the Koh-i-Nor had. The mode of sending the Koh-i-Nor to England was being debated by the Vice-regal Council at Government House, Sir John Lawerence, the Viceroy, presiding. One member of the Council asked very pertinently, "Where is it now?" Sir John said afterwards that his blood ran cold, for he remembered that for several nights the jewel had reposed in the pocket of his pyjama suit which was at that moment hanging up in the bathroom. Excusing himself for a few minutes he rushed into the bathroom, and, to his great relief, found it wrapped in a bit of tissue paper safe in his pocket!

Mightiest diamond of all both for size and significance, is the Cullinan. Uncut, it weighed 3,025 carats and measured $4\frac{1}{2}$ inches across; split in two, as it was by command of King Edward VII, it is still the world's biggest brilliant. And though the youngest of all historic gems—it was mined in Pretoria only in 1905—its history so far is more worthy than that which any of its elders can boast. For it was presented to King Edward in commemoration of the granting of self-government to the Transvaal, and no sordid or ignoble associations besmirch its fame. True, as a preliminary to a career of pomp and circumstance it travelled from South Africa to England in an ordinary wooden box consigned to the post without any special declaration whatever, but that was done to bluff some expert thieves who were known to be on the look-out for it, an episode which rather heightens than lessens the glamour of the jewel. Especially as the watching thieves actually did confiscate another box ostentatiously registered and insured.

Though its greatest occasion so far has been when, divided, it adorned the Imperial crown and topped the royal sceptre at King George's coronation, the Cullinan diamond will go down to history as having been first worn by a queen. For, coming as it did three years after King Edward's accession, there was little likelihood of it adding to the lustre of State ceremonial during his reign unless it was displayed by Queen Alexandra, and so King Edward had the two pieces into which the jewel had been split mounted for his consort to wear.

Great as is the British royal treasure of diamonds, it might have been very much greater had not Queen Victoria, after nine years litigation, reluctantly surrendered to the King of Hanover the fifty thousand pounds worth of such gems which George III had bought for Queen Charlotte's adornment at his coronation. Not that there was any stone of remarkable size and quality among them. But their number enabled this queen to wear at one of her birthday receptions a petticoat with "stripes of diamonds down it and fastened at the bottom with a large double row of diamonds."

b 9

Their number, too, probably accounted for the construction of the jewel cabinet which the King ordered to be made to contain them. Besides tiers of drawers behind outer doors, this jewel cabinet had a secret lift-up top, which formed a long shelf convenient for holding loose gems spread out for easy choice by Court Jeweller or Court Dressmaker. That cabinet, which was the work of the royal cabinet makers Vile & Cobb and is made of mahogany veneered with tulip, olive, and rosewood, now belongs to the Marquess of Cambridge to whom it descended from his grandmother Princess Mary Duchess of Teck, mother of England's present queen.

THE DIAMOND

It is mined chiefly in South Africa, South America (Brazil), the Belgian Congo and India, and mostly cut in Amsterdam, Antwerp, London, Paris, and Kimberley.

The diamond derives its name from the word 'adamant' meaning 'unconquerable,' in token of the great hardness of the gem. It is not only the hardest of all precious stones, but it is the hardest substance in nature. Nothing but its own dust will polish it, and tools set with small diamonds cut it.

A diamond is not necessarily 'white.' Among the Russian Crown Jewels is a red diamond and in the Dresden Museum a green one. There used to be a yellow diamond among the Austrian Crown

Jewels, and you will find a cinnamon-pink diamond at the Victoria and Albert Museum, London,—all exceedingly valuable because rare. A blue diamond known to fame as the Hope diamond once enriched the Imperial Regalia of France.

The diamond cut in baguette style, that is, to produce a longish rectangular stone, is beloved by the modern woman. Her grandmother loved the 'brilliant,' which was the result of cutting a diamond with an eightside table and so as to yield fifty-eight facets in all. Eighteenth century women of fashion preferred the 'Briolette' which is a diamond cut pear-shaped and facetted all over.

Chapter II

RUBIES OF ROYAL HERITAGE

FATHOMS deep in the Atlantic Ocean lies a parure of rubies which, sixty or so years ago, gleamed like fire on the neck and arms of an empress. Mined in Burma, and a wedding present to Princess Charlotte of Belgium when she married the Archduke Maximilian of Austria, those rubies were part of the paraphernalia with which it was sought to impress the Mexicans when the royal couple accepted the throne of Mexico at the behest of Napoleon III of France. Alas for Imperial plans! Two years only did the Empress Charlotte wear her rubies in the southern continent; then civil strife sent her scurrying back to Europe to seek Napoleon's aid for her harassed husband. But for that fruitless errand, which ended in sixty years of dementia for her and speedy assassination for Maximilian, the fate of the rubies might have been different. Left behind in the palace of Chalpultepec, they never came into their royal owner's possession again. Instead, after the fall of the Mexican Empire they found their way into the great Republican family de Madero, there to enhance the charms of its dark-eyed daughters till the coming of the 1908 Revolution. Then a hurried flight, a passage booked on an eastbound liner, the rubies stowed away in the purser's safe, and a wild storm in Chesapeake Bay to seal the fate of those gems for all time,—unless divers can salvage the shipwrecked treasure.

The rubies of Burma! Hindu mythology attributes their origin to a drop of blood spilled by the powerful Asura in combat with that other great enemy of the gods, the King of Lanka. It is a legend easier to believe in Bond Street or the Rue de la Paix than sixty miles north of Mandalay, at Moguk, where the ruby-bearing earth abounds. None but trained eyes can pick a ruby mid the mass of shingle tipped by a coolie on to a gem-sorter's table.

England is the country among western nations that possesses the ruby, or rather, spinel, with the longest European pedigree, the one which has place of honour in the King's State crown and was given to the Black Prince by the King of Castile nearly five hundred years ago. But Russia has long owned a bigger one, that which is the size of a pigeon's egg and the only coloured gem in the diadem made for the coronation of Catherine the Great.

There are two stories about the acquisition of that ruby spinel. One says it was bought for the Tzar Alexis Michailovitch by the Muscovite Ambassador to China, who gave 2,672 roubles for it in Peking; the other story says it cost "a load of gold ingots." At all events, polished but not cut, the gem remains where Jerémie Pozier the famous French jeweller placed it more than a century and a half ago, that is, just below the diamond cross at the top of the State crown; and it has not yet been listed among the Imperial Russian Treasure a Soviet Government is anxious to turn into cash.

Russian royalties' liking for coloured gems has always been pronounced. A psychological reason could probably be found for this—the same that accounted in bygone days for the gilded domes and spires of Russia's historic churches. Human beings naturally crave colour, and in a country wrapped in snow for at least four months of the year, it might well be that such a craving found expression in a passion for wearing precious stones of various hues, as well as in painting house roofs red and church spires the hue of a tropical sun.

South of the Volga the most celebrated rubies of royal heritage are those which Queen Marie of Roumania had from her mother, a Russian Tzar's daughter, who, in marrying an English queen's second son, became Duchess of Edinburgh and died Duchess of Saxe-Coburg-Gotha.

But how rarely the Roumanian queen wears her rubies! Or seems likely to do so in future. For she has lately handed them over to her youngest daughter the Princess Ileana. At least so rumour said in Bucharest at the time of that Princess's marriage with the Count von Hapsburg. "They will suit Ileana's dark beauty better than my English fairness," her Majesty is reported to have said.

14

Perhaps that is the secret of the ruby's eclipse in
Europe—there may be more blondes than brun-
ettes hereabouts now. But to such olive-skinned
queens as there have been in the western world
the ruby has made strong appeal. It was so with
the creole Josephine de Beauharnais who became
Empress of France and to whom Napoleon gave
a set of rubies as an ease to divorcement. But
were they? One wonders. To have a present appraised in terms of cash cannot be pleasing to the
recipient. Writing to Josephine at Malmaison the
Emperor said "The set of rubies—this will cost
me quite four hundred thousand francs. I will
have it valued as I do not wish to be cheated by the
jeweller."

As royal gifts rubies take a high place in the
hierarchy of precious stones. Queen Victoria was
the recipient of several. One, that came to her a
few years earlier than the Koh-i-Nor diamond, is
famed for having decked the lovely consort of
Shah Jehan, he who built to his beloved's memory
that most exquisite of buildings, the Taj Mahal.
But before then this ruby had belonged to another
famous eastern ruler, the Mogul Emperor Jehan-
gir, who, in spite of his lady's remonstrances,
carved his name upon it, saying "This jewel will
more certainly hand down my name to posterity
than any written history. The house of Taimur
may fall, but as long as there is a king this jewel
will be his." And so events have proved, although

the king-emperor in whose keeping the ruby now is, abides in the west.

Out of India, too, came an uncut ruby treasured by Queen Victoria till her death because it had been a personal gift from the Maharani of Cooch Behar in the days when Indian ladies of high degree were first presented at the Court of St. James. Now that jewel belongs to Princess Alice countess of Athlone, who had it from her mother the Duchess of Albany to whom Queen Victoria bequeathed it. Set round with diamonds the ruby makes a lovely corsage ornament, which Princess Alice often wears on State occasions and always when she is likely to meet the Maharani or any of her family.

Nor is Queen Mary without rubies with a history. Under the will of the late Countess Torby wife of the Grand Duke Michael of Russia her Majesty received a ruby brooch and pendant that had been given to the Countess by her Imperial brothers-in-law and originally had been chosen for the Empress Alexandra.

Pinned on the corsage of a pale gold satin evening gown and matched by ruby earrings, that ruby brooch out of Imperial Russia has recently been immortalised in paint. For it is Queen Mary's chief jewel in the portrait Mr David Jagger did of her in 1932, a portrait which was hung in the Royal Academy of that year and is now gracing the Royal Bethlehem Hospital, presented thereto by Lord Wakefield.

Among bygone queens-consort it seems to have been Anne, wife of James I who had the greatest predilection for rubies, probably because she hailed from that land of snow and ice and long dark winters,—Denmark. Certainly, of the nigh upon forty thousand pounds (£40,000) she spent in a little more than ten years with the Court Jeweller George Herriot, much of it went in ruby-gemmed personal ornaments. Her Majesty's ruby rings especially were numerous and expensive; and she had, besides, many ruby bracelets, to say nothing of ruby pendants. This queen seems also to have worn rubies strung together much as present-day royal ladies wear pearls, for the said Herriot's Accounts and Vouchers contain various items for "Piercing rubies;" one was for "piercing twelve rock rubies." She even had a girdle of rubies in the form of roses, an ornament her son Charles I quickly sold when it came into his possession at his mother's death.

Indeed, if Anne had not "left a world of brave jewels behind" and all to Charles, the next queen-consort, the French Henrietta Maria, would never have been able to raise on royal jewels two millions sterling in one year. Not even with the King's great collar of rubies—a crown possession—put at her disposal to raise funds for Charles's war-mongering ventures.

Many of Anne's rubies were 'balas' rubies, really a rosetinted spinel mined in Ceylon and very

17

much the rage in Stuart England. One of the gifts of Mary Queen of Scots to Darnley consisted of seventy-one buttons "great, middle-size, and small," each "set with a balas ruby"; and in the inventory of her own jewels mention is made of two costly ruby chains formed of twelve pieces each set with two rubies, two diamonds, and twenty-four pearls.

The French royalties of that period were also partial to balas rubies. When the Queen of Navarre made her will leaving to her daughter all her jewels "except those in the hands of Queen Elizabeth of England," she named a large balas ruby set in a ring which she gave to her son for an heirloom in the crown of Navarre.

Rubies have figured in poetry as much as any precious stone except pearls, probably because, as a cynic once said, the word was more euphonious and easier to rhyme, than the names of other gems. That, maybe, was true of Chaucer in the Knight's Tale when he described the King of Thrace as having a short mantle

"bret-full of rubies red as fire sparkling"

but surely there was historic chapter and verse for Sir Walter Scott to go upon in writing of King James before the battle of Flodden

"His bonnet all of crimson fair,
was buttoned with a ruby rare."

The ruby is known to have been a favourite stone with gem engravers of classical times, though there is little tangible evidence to support such knowledge, in spite of the fact that wealthy citizens of Imperial Rome were ardent collectors of the work of famous old Greek gem engravers. The two best known engraved rubies dating back to that period are the one owned by the Duke of Marlborough and bearing a representation of the head of the dog Sirius with a collar round its neck; and the ruby in the Devonshire collection which bears a figure of Venus Victrix cut in intaglio.

Very different were the subjects depicted by gem engravers in Asia. The dragon was and is their favourite device, especially for the ruby, probably because that gem so engraved is believed by Hindus to ensure health, wealth, and a joyous nature to the owner. Even minus any engraving a ruby is held in high esteem as a talisman, especially if it be a Brahmin ruby, that is, one belonging to the highest of the five castes into which Hindus classify rubies. A Brahmin ruby is supposed to safeguard its wearer from all evil no matter how closely beset by enemies. Some such belief was connected with the ruby in England in the Middle Ages. But the stone, whether set in ring or bracelet, had to be worn on the left side if its efficacy was to extend to its owner's house, garden, or fruit trees. So the quaint fourteenth century writer Sir John Mandeville has left on record.

Perhaps the rarest ruby known to fame is one owned by a member of the Bengal Legislative Council, a gem that was the talk of jewellers the world over a few years ago. For inside it, deep down behind a scarlet cloud, there appears the tiny image of a dark-skinned man robed in white, his head swathed in a white turban.

Except as a freak there is no explaining that portrait-ruby. But as soon as its existence became known in the western world it was listed by connoisseurs as a gem worth going far to see should it ever come into a jewel mart this side the Euphrates.

THE RUBY

IT COMES from Burma, Siam, and Ceylon and is a coloured variety of the mineral corundum. The most highly prized is the so-called pigeon-blood ruby—a deep rich red very slightly tinged with mauve. Only Burma yields that kind of gem and rarely of any size above five carats, although on Armistice Day 1919 one was found that weighed forty-two carats.

Appropriately named 'Peace Ruby' it fetched three hundred thousand (300,000) rupees uncut. In cutting it was reduced to twenty-four carats, but even so still ranks as a rarity.

Siamese rubies are darker than the Burmese, and are characterised by a purple-brown tinge which renders them less saleable in Europe than in Asia. Yet only experts can detect this tinge. They look, too, for what is known as 'silk' in a ruby, that is, patches of fine parallell lines in a Burmese ruby and patches of little speckles in a Siamese ruby. Detection of 'silk' in a ruby is not possible by the naked eye; a magnifying glass must be used.

A Ceylon ruby is the palest kind of ruby, and has a very limpid brilliancy. It is discovered in the gravel of river beds and the courses of mountain torrents; like the Siamese ruby is chiefly bought by eastern peoples.

A spinel looks like a ruby to the naked eye and is often miscalled one. But if put under a jeweller's magnifying glass a spinel only shows one colour whereas a ruby shows two. Moreover a spinel is not a corundum mineral but a totally different kind of crystal.

Chapter III

PEARLS OF GREAT PRICE

WHEN Cleopatra crushed that pearl to powder for the wine cup she drank with Mark Anthony, she made a sacrifice to love which the modern maiden would consider senseless waste. For nowadays we count our pearls more precious than diamonds, and if, as the experts say, the world's pearl fisheries are rapidly becoming exhausted, then these gems will go up in value.

Some pearls there are with a history that puts them beyond price. Such are the pearls Queen Mary is wearing in that portrait of her which hangs in the Garter Room at Windsor, a painting done by Sir William Llewellyn, R.A. in 1914. Known at Court as the "Hanoverian" pearls, they were, early in Queen Victoria's reign and by decision of the House of Lords, "vested as heirlooms for ever in the British Crown."

Before then it had seemed likely that the Duke of Cumberland might get them. For, on the severance of the kingdoms of Great Britain and Hanover from under one sovereignty, this uncle of Queen Victoria claimed all the jewels which had come to England with George the First and thereafter added to, these pearls included.

Luckily there was ample proof that the pearls had originally gone from England with the eldest daughter of James the First, the Princess Elizabeth, when she married the Elector Palatine of the Rhine, a Stuart ancestress from whom Queen Victoria was more directly descended than was the Duke of Cumberland. So the "Hanoverian" pearls were not among the jewels the Crown lawyers conceded might go back to the little German Court on the banks of the Leine.

But the dispute about their ownership always rankled with Queen Victoria and was the chief reason why she seldom wore them, and when she did it was chiefly as a delicate hint to visiting potentates of the power and glory of the British monarchy.

One such occasion her Majesty noted in her diary. "I dressed in a smart morning dress with my large pearls," she wrote apropos of the visit to Windsor of the Shah Naser-el-Din of Persia.

And evidently that eastern ruler was duly impressed. Indeed his eyes were seemingly so riveted on the pearls while he was slipping the ribbon of a Persian Order over her Britannic Majesty's head and shoulders, that he knocked the royal lady's cap askew. "But," recorded the royal diarist, "the Grand Vizier came to the rescue."

Thus the Grand Vizier also got a close-up of the famous pearls to stimulate his pen when writing the official reports he sent home of his Imperial master's doings abroad.

Though the Hanoverian pearls were rarely seen by anyone during Queen Victoria's lifetime it was different when they came to Queen Alexandra as part of the Crown Jewels. This royal lady loved the pearls for their sheer beauty, and took every opportunity of wearing them in public. From the day when, in great ropes, they cascaded to her knees over the golden embroideries of her Coronation robe, Queen Alexandra was rarely seen without them when in ceremonial attire.

And King Edward was glad to have it so. Still there was one occasion when those pearls caused him to fret and fume and do something he abhorred—that is, be late for a public appointment.

It all happened in a flash. Queen Alexandra was stepping into the State Coach to go with the King to Westminster for the State Opening of Parliament when the pearls caught in the woodwork, a string broke, and scatter went scores of gems, mostly between coach wheels and horses' hoofs. And were not royal horses the well-trained animals they are, some of the Hanoverian pearls might, like Cleopatra's, have been crushed to powder, though in a very different cause. As it was, they were all safely collected, but not without much loss of dignity on the part of those royal footmen who had to grovel in quest of the rolling gems.

Hanoverian—Stuart—Tudor—French—such is the lineage in reverse order, of those famous pearls. Or, at all events, the majority of them. For the jewels with which James the First of England

ELIZABETH, ELECTRESS PALATINE AND QUEEN OF BOHEMIA, WEARING
THE CABLE OF FAMOUS PEARLS.

From the original painting by Van Miereveldt in the National Portrait
Gallery.

To face page 24.]

endowed his eldest daughter when she married the Elector Palatine of the Rhine, included most of the pearls that had belonged to the last Tudor sovereign, the redoubtable Elizabeth. And she, as history tells, paid £3,000 for the pearls of Mary Queen of Scots who had acquired her collection of such gems in France, either as gifts from her husband the Dauphin, or from her royal mother-in-law Catherine de Medicis. Indeed had Catherine had her way Mary's pearls would have returned to the country whence they came; she actually instructed her Ambassador at the English Court to buy them if possible. But the Queen Mother of France never had any chance against the Queen-Regnant of England who had been complimented with the first offer of the pearls and was allowed to purchase them at her own price.

Many times and oft have those pearls been painted, thus leaving to posterity interesting records of the varying ways in which their royal owners have worn them. One such seventeenth century record is Van Mireveldt's portrait of 'Elizabeth, Electress Palatine, Queen of Bohemia' which hangs in the National Portrait Gallery, London. But having looked upon that picture showing the pearls massed like cables round a waist and chest encased in heavy brocaded velvet, one turns thankfully to Luke Fildes' portrait of Queen Alexandra wearing the same gems set against the alluring beauty of bared throat and shoulders.

Come with me to Italy and I will show you another royal portrait that reveals the pictorial possibilities of pearls worn in the modern manner. In the Quirinale, at Rome, it hangs, a painting done by Gardigiani of the late Queen Margherita wearing the famous furlong of pearls she bequeathed to her grandson the Crown Prince in trust for his bride.

Few royal necks have been so completely hidden by pearls as this one, few royal shoulders been cascaded over by such a rippling stream of what in ancient days were regarded as "tears of celestial beings."

This Italian royal treasure of pearls has not always been as great as it is now, not by as much as thirty-two strings, each just long enough to fit round the base of Queen Margherita's throat. For when, as Princess of Savoy, she married the then Italian Crown Prince and donned for the first time the historic pearl necklace bequeathed by her husband's mother Queen Maria Adelaide for the bride of Italy's Heir-apparent, she acquired a royal ornament of comparatively small value, though one rich in romance. But an enamoured bridegroom soon set about remedying the necklace's shortcomings by promising his bride an additional string on every aniversary of their life together.

Hence the wonderful furlong of pearls that Queen Margherita possessed when King Humbert died, and which Princess Marie José of Belgium found awaiting her to wear when she went to Italy as the bride of the present Crown Prince.

Pearls appealed little to Russian royalties although the engagement ring of the last Tzaritza was gemmed with pink pearls and matched by a necklace of similar gems from her fiancé. But then, this Empress was not of Slav ancestry and never truly appreciated anyone who was—except her husband.

Her predecessors showed no partiality for pearls unless such gems were allied to diamonds, a reason, probably, why so few strings or ropes of pearls are listed and illustrated in the catalogue of the Imperial Treasure issued by the Soviet Government.

The best of such ornaments—a necklace which had belonged to the Tzaritza Feodorovna and composed of 182 well-assorted pearls in three graduated strings held by a clasp of diamonds—makes poor showing beside a circlet of thirteen pear-shaped pearls each rimmed in diamonds, which another Imperial lady used to wear. The finest pearls Russia ever possessed are, of course, in the Imperial Crown,—two rows of big and perfectly matched oriental pearls flanking the ridge where the rising arch of massed diamonds divides.

Sometimes Imperial pearls "come down in the world." That may be said to have happened to the historic Hapsburg pearls, the wonderful rope which the Empress Marie Theresa of Austria used to wear wound several times round her throat and then looped and swathed across her ample bosom, according to Meytens' many portraits of her which hang at Schonbrunn in Vienna. For three hundred years those pearls were part of the Austrian Imperial treasure, decking among other empresses of renown the lovely but neurasthenic Elizabeth who early forsook the Court of her consort Francis Joseph to go wandering through Europe in quest of health. Now the Hapsburg pearls are the prized possession of a millionaire racehorse owner, who lives most of the year at Cannes. A revolution was the cause of their drop from glory, but in their descent they at least acquired a glamour no other pearls can claim. For they were sold to buy the airplane and furnish the funds by which the last of the Hapsburg monarchs, the ex-emperor Charles, attempted his spectacular re-entry into Hungary.

Also along the Mediterranean littoral lives another lady born neither royal nor 'great' who possesses another defunct queen's pearls, those which Marie Antoinette wore with such incomparable grace at Versailles. Bought with the Vanderbilt millions to enhance the charm of the American wife of England's eighth Duke of Marlborough, those pearls made many a sensation at the Court of St. James during the brief and brilliant Edwardian era. And though their owner has since renounced her coronet to become merely Madame Jacques Balsan, the famous pearls have not lost lustre, literally or figuratively.

At Lou Sueil, the chateau near Eze in the south of France which Colonel and Madame Balsan built soon after their marriage, the pearls are perhaps more glamorous with romance than ever they were, for now they are back in the land where they first made history.

East of Suez lies what is claimed to be the finest collection of pearls in the world, that belonging to the Maharajah of Baroda. And well it might be, seeing that thirty-five necklaces of several strings each, and each ranging from one thousand to twenty thousand pounds in value, are but a fraction of the whole. On State occasions the Maharajah—for in the east it is the man who wears the jewels—dons a seven string necklace of two hundred and eighty graduated pearls that is valued at over half a million sterling. And he possesses also the famous £10,000 pearl known as the Paragon, a round lovely gem of great lustre weighing forty-eight grains. Indeed, what with pearls and diamonds and other precious stones, mounted and unmounted, it takes twenty pages of foolscap typescript to list—not describe—the Baroda jewels. Yet not a single solitaire gleams about their owner's person when he is in Europe. Then, at least, his wife, the Maharani, eclipses him, with jewels at her ears and on her fingers.

One of these days it is more than likely that there will appear in the western world pearls that have girdled an empress in her coffin. For the rulers of China have always been buried with splendour, and when the last of them—the Dowager Empress Tzu-Hzi—died, her brittle bones were wrapped in gorgeous raiment and nine times round her body was wound a rope of pearls valued at £1,250,000. So her celebrated eunuch Li-Lien-Ying recorded in his diary. And since then the Chinese Press has told of the desecration of royal tombs and the offering of loot therefrom for sale in Tientsin. So, putting two and two together, it is easy to predict that when peace comes to the East, more will be heard in the West of some of the Imperial pearls that were buried with the notoriously masterful Manchu Empress of China in the first year of the present century.

Although pearls with a history, especially royal history, can always command big prices when the turn of fortune's wheel pitches them into the open market, it is a pearl's colour, other things being equal, that determines most women's choice in such gems. And that choice is largely governed by the natural flesh tints of the pearl's prospective wearer. Rarely do you find South American women wearing the same kind of pearls as English women, the former preferring yellowish pearls to suit their tawny skins, while the latter choose the whitest pearls they can get as a match to their fair flesh. The French aristocrats would wear none but pearls of a live warm rosy tint until the Empress Eugenie set a fashion for black pearls, by showing how the lustrous dark perfection of such pearls heightened the allure of her beautiful throat.

The most coveted black pearls have a greenish tinge and come chiefly from the Paumotus and the Gulf of California, although those beloved by the Empress Eugenie hailed from that part of the Pacific round about the Fiji Islands.

Of all the jewels the last Empress of the French possessed at the zenith of her power and glory, those black pearls were, with the exception of certain emeralds, the only gems she was able to preserve for her heirs. And she bequeathed them to Princess Marie Clotilde, the only daughter of the French Pretender Prince Victor Napoleon, by his marriage with the wealthy Princess Clementine of Belgium.

THE PEARL

As EVERY woman knows, a pearl is the product of an oyster. Luckily for her, there are seven kinds of oyster which will obligingly perform that miracle. And such oysters are mostly got from tropical seas, especially those which lap the continent of Asia.

The Persian Gulf is the most prolific in 'shell' that yields the finest pearls, though probably the biggest pearls are taken off North Australia and the Paumotus in the South Pacific.

Even so, there are pearls obtained within sight of Ceylon, India, China, and Japan, which are well worth any woman's wearing.

Pearl oysters are dived for. The greatest number of pearl divers in the world still stick to the primitive methods and dive with nothing on but a loin cloth, and no apparatus beyond two ropes, a stone to weigh one of the ropes, and a net bag. Such a pearl diver stays under water about seventy seconds. Then his breath gives out and he signals to be hauled to the surface. Along the Australian coast there are pearl divers who spend much longer periods on the ocean bed because they go down wearing helmets and armour.

Not all pearl divers are men. Or have not always been. Round about the Torres Straits diving for pearls used to be undertaken by native women, and capital divers they made.

Pearl stringers, however, are all women. Those who practise their rather exclusive craft in London, work for world-famed jewellers and thus are often entrusted with priceless pearls from the collection of visiting Indian princes and other eastern potentates. Or they may be sent into the depths of the country to re-string some historic heirloom pearls belonging to one of our oldest English families.

Not all pearls come from the depths of tropical

seas. Some hail from the quieter waters of Irish and Scottish rivers. But such pearls are mussel pearls, and only fetch a fair, not a great, price. One found not long ago in an Irish river realised fifty pounds. And there is an even more valuable one, found in Scottish waters, set in the Crown Jewels of Scotland now reposing in Edinburgh Castle.

A river pearler is not a diver but a wader. And he goes equipped with a cleft stick and a pearling-glass, this latter a square box with a glass bottom which, when laid on the surface of the water, shows up the river bed quite distinctly.

Chapter IV
EMERALDS OF IMPERIAL SPLENDOUR

WHEN the City of Paris presented a diadem of emeralds to the Empress Eugenie soon after her marriage to Napoleon III, it paid more than a tribute to beauty—it testified to the emerald's high rank in the hierarchy of precious stones.

So did the Empress herself when she appeared at Court in a dress of gold tissue embroidered in large emeralds enlivened with rivulets of diamonds. Indeed the emerald was this royal lady's favourite coloured gem. As well it might be, since its green lustre enhanced her blonde beauty of fair hair and milk white flesh. At her ears and on her head, round her throat and wrists, pinning her corsage and buckling those white satin slippers which she never wore more than once, emeralds gleamed scarcely less often than diamonds. And fetched nearly as much when the Imperial collection of jewels was dispersed at Christie's just sixty years ago. For one little 'lot' of three emerald brooches the bidding ran up to over three thousand guineas.

That earlier French empress, Josephine, wife of a greater Napoleon than Eugenie's consort, also loved emeralds. There is a story told that when Josephine was having her portrait done on enamel by the celebrated miniaturist, Isabey, just before

34

CATHERINE II OF RUSSIA.

EMPRESS JOSEPHINE WEARING HER FAMOUS PARURE
OF EMERALDS AND PEARLS.

From the original painting by Gerard in the Château
de la Malmaison.

To face page 34.]

her divorce was publicly announced, she chose to be painted wearing emeralds "to denote the undying freshness of my grief," she remarked to the artist. "But," she added, "let the emeralds be surrounded with diamonds to portray the purity of my love." Usually, however, Josephine preferred her emeralds allied to pearls, and in that respect she resembled Lollia Paulina wife of the Roman Emperor Caligula, who had a set of pearls and emeralds worth the equivalent of two million dollars.

The particular parure of emeralds and pearls which Napoleon gave Josephine on his return from his victorious Italian campaign the Empress had immortalised in paint. Necklace, earrings, corsage ornament and high fender-like tiara—all are there in the Gerard portrait of the Empress Josephine which hangs at Malmaison for anyone to see. Up to a few years ago the necklace in that parure and exactly as Josephine had worn it, was the prized heirloom possession of her grand-niece the Baroness Surcough. Alas! thieves came one night to the Baroness's Paris flat and the historic ornament vanished for ever in its recognisable form. Broken up, as stolen jewels quickly are, the gems which composed the necklace are probably now enhancing the charms of several non-royal ladies in various parts of the civilized world. But necessarily without any documentary evidence as to pedigree, such as went with the Wittlesbach emeralds in the collection of the Bavarian Crown Jewels sold at Christie's recently.

The Wittlesbach emeralds, nine in number, fetched big prices considering that they were unset. Five out of the nine were sold for a total of £14,500, the top price being £5,600 for one of oblong shape weighing 53.35 carats. A Parisian firm of jewellers bought it, but rumour said they were acting for an Indian Maharajah who collects emeralds, and preferably those with a royal history made in Europe.

French royalties during the First Empire were all rather partial to emeralds, and Napoleon's favourite sister the Princess Pauline, created an even bigger sensation with her collection of such gems than did the Empress Josephine. For Pauline specialised in girdles, a fashion that became her perfect figure better than it did the less perfect form of Josephine.

Not that all the emeralds Pauline flaunted in that daring style were real. One of her most wonderful ceintures was composed of false emeralds surrounded by real diamonds, a piece of jewelry that cost her thirteen thousand francs and looked worth a million!

Naturally that belt's beauty and its wearer's extravagance set all Paris talking; nor did the talk lessen when the truth about the stones leaked out. Yet if anyone was chagrined it certainly was not the Princess Pauline. She got almost as much enjoyment from bluffing the censorious know-alls as from the commotion the ornament caused when she first wore it.

A hundred years later emeralds were all the rage at the Russian Court. The Grand Duchess Elizabeth Feodorovna especially, was famous for the number and value of her emeralds, and for the form in which she had them set as personal ornaments. She liked them best combined with diamonds, the diamonds framed in silver, the emeralds so set that they quivered whenever the wearer made the slightest movement.

One three-piece suite which this Grand-Duchess had made of Columbian emeralds and South African diamonds—a plastron, necklace, and diadem—was remarkable for the alternating scrolls and Empire bows dominating the head-piece. A relic of departed power and glory, that emerald parure was among the jewels that lay hidden in the Armoury of the Kremlin for four years after the Bolshevik Revolution in 1917. Now it is part of the Soviet Government's carefully guarded treasures, along with the finest known emerald in existence, a wonderful stone weighing 136 carats.

A bigger 'piece' of emerald there used to be among the Russian treasure, but it was more an objet d'art than a jewel, being a representation of the Chinese Goddess of Mercy, Kwan-yin, leading a child by the hand, the two figures carved from a single lump of emerald mined in the Ural

Mountains 150 years ago. An amazing example of lapidarian skill, that emerald 'Goddess' was among the first precious things the Soviet Government decided to sell. And it was brought from Leningrad to Paris in nothing more secure than an ordinary Gladstone bag!

Emeralds had no great vogue in England during the nineteenth century although Queen Victoria possessed several fine ones, including two that had been sent to her as a gift by the Imam of Muscat. Indeed the only emeralds of renown chronicled as being worn at Drawing-Rooms and other State functions were those of the Duchess of Teck, gems now belonging to Queen Mary who had them from her brother the late Prince Francis of Teck.

To those emeralds attaches the intriguing legend that they were won in a lottery by Queen Mary's grandmother the Duchess of Cambridge, the royal lady to whom the Hanoverian Crown Jewels were sent for safety in England when Prussia declared war on Hanover.

Be that as it may those emeralds now rim one of Queen Mary's high diamond crowns and space double links of diamonds in a necklace that has 'tie' ends weighted, one with an emerald and the other with a diamond. And when her Majesty wears these heirloom gems, other emeralds, more recently acquired, stud the royal ears and gleam in a magnificent corsage ornament. For the Queen

THE CHINESE GODDESS OF MERCY, KWAN YIN,
CARVED OUT OF THE LARGEST KNOWN PIECE OF
EMERALD.

By courtesy of Messrs. Wartski, Regent Street.

JADE RINGS AND THREE COLOUR BRACELET.
By courtesy of Messrs. Liberty & Co., Ltd., Regent
Street.

To face page 38.

likes her jewels en suite, and being the connoisseur she is of precious stones, saw to it that her newer emeralds matched as near as possible the ones which by family reckoning might reasonably be called old.

Two reasons are sometimes given for the social eclipse of the emerald in England during the nineteenth century, one being Queen Victoria's passion for diamonds and the other the classic dedication of the gem to Venus. Yet besides its astrological association with the love passion, the emerald was credited with the power to sharpen the wits, quicken the intelligence, and make its possessor economical,—all qualities rated high by the Victorians. So probably there was another and more tangible reason, say scarcity, and the eagerness of eastern potentates to snap up the best of the output of the emerald mines of Columbia in South America.

Anyhow, whatever the cause of the emerald's nineteenth century fall from favour, the reason for its twentieth century rise to eminence is in some measure due to the gem-engraver. Pedigree emeralds from royal collections are only for multi-millionaires' womenfolk, but carved and engraved emeralds of present-day craftsmanship come within the reach of less-rich men's wives.

True, such gems would hardly be of the calibre of the engraved emerald Queen Mary sometimes wears as a pendant, a jewel which was a gift to her when in India with King George for the Coronation Durbar; but they can be none the less beautiful. The modern designer of jewels is showing himself to be a sculptor in spirit as well as an exceedingly fine lapidary, and already his work is being appraised by discriminating collectors as the museum pieces of the future.

Meanwhile betrothals and weddings in royal and aristocratic circles bear best witness to the emerald's return to favour. The herald of that return was the choice in 1922 by the King's only daughter, of an emerald engagement ring; the proof was the number of emeralds among the wedding gifts of the Queen's niece Lady May Cambridge when she married Captain Abel Smith in 1931. And for further testimony there have been the Royal Courts at Buckingham Palace when among the wearers of emeralds has been the youthful Duchess of Northumberland.

Spain possesses several fine emeralds among her Crown Jewels and might be possessing many more had Hernando Cortez acted on Queen Isabella's hint and handed over to her all he brought back from his conquest of Mexico. But being about to marry, and deeming a big, rich slice of a continent enough of a gift for any queen, Cortez kept back some of his spoils for his bride. Notably five rare emeralds carved, so legend says, into the semblance of a rose, a fish, a hunting horn, a bell clapper and a tiny cup. Naturally the queen resented being denied such lovely ornaments, and it is hardly to be wondered at, if, in consequence, Cortez lost favour at Court.

Away in Asia there is also a rising tide of interest in emeralds. But hardly for the same reason. All the world used to be thrilled by tales of the fabulous jewels of Persia—of sacks full of sapphires, tubs full of rubies, tanks crammed with turquoises, to say nothing of cupboards choked with belts and gauntlets massed with pearls, swords scabbarded with diamonds and goblets rimmed with emeralds. Shah Pahlevi has recently corrected all that though not to the extent of disillusioning the western world completely. The strong room at the Palace of Teheran is still much of an Aladdin's cave. But its gleaming contents have been tabulated and a value put upon them by European experts called in for the purpose. It has been said that if the state of the national finances suggested the valuation of the Persian Crown Jewels, then national pride demanded the broadcasting far and wide of the expert's estimate that of emeralds alone there was a bulk weight of thirteen pounds, while the largest of those gems was valued at £15,600.

As for Turkey, or rather the Angora Republic, there a renewed interest in the emerald has been stimulated by Mustapha Kemal's command that the Jewel House of bygone Sultans should be thrown open for public visitation and the most

d

gorgeous contents photographed for circulation in the western world. One wondrous exhibit, a huge uncut emerald eleven inches round, four and a quarter inches long, and one and a half inches thick, used to hang as a tassel attached to a large heart-shaped pendant of pure gold suspended above Sultan Ahmid's head as he sat on a throne of gold.

What a jewel to deck the wife of an American multi-millionaire should it ever be sold to replenish the coffers of the Angora Government! Before that happens, however, it is much more likely that an official raid will be made on the emeralds in the Imperial aigrettes, for such gems could easily be replaced by aunthetic replicas without any loss of effectiveness. In the old days of the Ottoman Empire jewelled aigrettes were part of the insignia of royalty, and some of the most ornate worn by the splendour-loving Sultans, were studded with large emeralds in conjunction with small diamonds.

Nearer the Danube than the Bosphorus rest some of the finest cabochon emeralds known in the world to-day. They were the marriage gift of a king to his bride, and chosen, so Court gossip said, because his Majesty had been surfeited with the sight of the marvellous pearls his prospective female 'in-laws' had everlastingly worn during his visit of courtship. At all events the statuesque beauty and fair colouring of Queen Marie of Jugo-

Slavia are well set off by the emeralds King Alexander had ready for her when she arrived from Bucharest to be married to him in Belgrade. Set Byzantine fashion in diadem, necklace, and long pendant earrings, those cabochon emeralds have had no more enthusiastic admirer than the Duchess of York, who saw them when she visited Belgrade with the Duke for the christening of the Infant Crown Prince.

THE EMERALD

It comes from Columbia, a State in north-west South America, from Russia in the vicinity of the Ural Mountains, from North Carolina and from Australia.

The finest are the Columbian stones, clear and transparent and crystallised in six-sided prisms; the least fine the Australian emeralds. That is because they are apt to be cloudy, a fault the Queen remarked upon when she was shown the first consignment of Australian emeralds at the 1928 British Industries Fair.

The emerald belongs to the beryl group of gems and gets its grass-green colour from oxide of chromium. It ranks third in the scale of mineral hardness, the diamond being first and the ruby second.

Long ere the days of Spanish adventuring in South and Central America, the Columbian emerald mines had been discovered and worked by the

43

native Indians. The Spaniards speeded up the mining and hastened the marketing of the output. They were hard taskmasters and greedy, consequently the history of the emerald, like that of other precious stones, has many chapters compact of cruelty and rapacity.

Emeralds are not dug for in the bowels of the earth as the word 'mining' suggests to European ears. The workings are in the open on the mountain side, and the miner can glimpse the sky above him as he cuts through the black carbonaceous limestone.

The emerald is easy to imitate by means of a very thin layer of green gelatine imprisoned between two extremely fine pieces of colourless transparent quartz. Yet the imitation is easy to detect if a Beryloscope is used, and if the detective knows the characteristics to look for in order to distinguish the false from the real emerald. That knoweldge is as important as the Beryloscope itself, but not all jewellers possess it.

Chapter V
SAPPHIRES THAT HAVE MADE HISTORY

ONE bright November morning in the first decade of the present century there was a great gathering of crowned heads and other royalties, mostly foreign, at Wood Norton, near Evesham in leafy Worcestershire. Princess Louise, sister of Philippe Duke of Orleans, was being married to Prince Charles of Bourbon-Sicily. And in honour of the event, the hostess, the Duchess of Orleans, wore what is probably the most famous set of sapphires in history, jewels which had belonged to Queen Marie Antoinette of France.

Far removed from Worcestershire, England, are those sapphires now. An heirloom in the Bourbon-Orleans royal family, they came in due course to the present 'Pretender' to the French throne, the Duc de Guise, who lives most of the year at Palermo, in Sicily. And there it is that these historic sapphires have been oftenest worn of late. For since the Duke was exiled from France —automatically so, as soon as he succeeded his cousin as head of a family that had reigned in France—three of his children have married; and marriages are occasions of great pomp and circumstance with the Bourbons. Heirloom lace and heirloom jewels then make fine array. When the only son of the Duc de Guise wedded the Princess

45

Isabella of Braganza a couple of years ago, the Duchess wore the Marie Antoinette sapphires with a gown of ivory and gold lame and Point d'Alencon lace.

Mined in Siam and of a deep royal blue colour, such sapphires were more fancied in the eighteenth than in the nineteenth century. Which probably explains why the huge sapphire that acts as a socket for the diamond cross atop the orb made for Catherine the Great of Russia is of the same rich blue. Indeed the Russian Crown Jewels contain few sapphires that are otherwise. Those few were the choice of the last Tzaritza, who preferred the paler cornflower blue stone mined in Ceylon.

Sapphires seem to have been this Imperial lady's favourite gem, perhaps because they were akin in colour to her eyes. Or maybe because, among the many diadems she found awaiting her when she arrived in Russia as a bride, those set with sapphires were lighter in weight and more graceful in design than those gleaming with emeralds and rubies.

One diadem that became a favourite with this tragic-fated empress—it had been made for an earlier Tzaritza and was of Empire design—not only contained several large pear-shaped and oval sapphires, but had pale blue enamel introduced among the surrounding diamonds.

For occasions not demanding formal splendour this Tzaritza preferred to wear jewelled aigrettes,

46

and one in particular, shaped like a feather that had all its gems—five big sapphires and seventy-five small ones mixed with diamonds—mounted on fine wires so that with the slightest turn of the wearer's head they quivered and scintillated with entrancing effect.

Nowadays the Russian passion for coloured gems is well understood and keenly appreciated in England, but it was not so when Queen Victoria's second son, the Duke of Edinburgh, married the Grand Duchess Marie only daughter of Tzar Nicholas II. True, Queen Victoria did occasionally wear a necklace of sapphires—sometimes of rubies—when she held a Drawing-room, but she possessed nothing like the collection of sapphires, emeralds, and rubies her Russian daughter-in-law brought to this country. Indeed the value and magnificence of the new Duchess of Edinburgh's jewelry amazed the Court of St. James. So did the Duchess's way of housing her different sets of jewels. Not for them banishment to the darkness of leather cases stored away in the cavernous depths of a steel safe. They must be within their owner's range of vision and displayed so that their sparkle and colourful beauty could be enjoyed any minute of the day. So at Eastwell, where the Duke and Duchess of Edinburgh spent their early married life, a special jewel room was built out of the Duchess's bedroom, its walls lined with glass-cases fitted with velvet-covered shelves and stands like the showroom at Cartier's in Bond Street or Mauboussin's in the Rue de la Paix.

Only when her Royal Highness retired to rest at night were the glittering jewels blotted from her sight,—by iron shutters that clamped over all the cases. But never, day or night was that jewel room left unguarded. Special watchmen were always on duty every minute of every twenty-four hours.

If it needed a royal wedding to awaken nineteenth century England to the beauty and becomingness of coloured jewels, it was by a royal wedding that twentieth century England showed the measure of her appreciation of such gems. For, when the present monarch's only daughter married Viscount Lascelles the amount of sapphire-gemmed jewelry among the wedding gifts was remarkable. The King and Queen were especially lavish with such ornaments—a whole suite—tiara, necklace, earrings and corsage ornament—of sapphires allied to diamonds being their principal gift to their daughter. A true cornflower blue those sapphires are, and of a size and sparkle that seemed to hypnotise most of the forty thousand beholders who paid their shillings to view the Royal wedding gifts displayed in St. James's Palace while the Princess and her husband were honeymooning in Italy. Even the Prince of Wales, then out of England, sent his sister sapphires—in the form of a bracelet. And, in memory of the time when, booted and spurred she had had her first run with hounds on the Sandringham estate, the Royal bride accepted a brooch of sapphires and diamonds from the members of the West Norfolk Hunt.

All of which stimulated interest in sapphires tremendously, and led to youth and beauty appropriating a gem that had long been relegated to dowagers and their adornment. Thereafter for quite a decade, scarcely an aristocratic maiden became engaged but chose a sapphire for her betrothal ring and let her relatives know that any prospective wedding gifts of jewels should follow the same trend as to gems. When the Lady Anne Cavendish, daughter of the Duke and Duchess of Devonshire, married Mr Henry Hunloke a one-time royal page, she received, among other jewels from the bridegroom, a sapphire and diamond bracelet and a huge sapphire and diamond cross. And when the Duke of Westminster was about to marry as his third wife the daughter of Sir Frederick Ponsonby, he showered sapphires galore upon his future Duchess, so that she might have plenty of ornaments to match the sapphire, about half the size of a postage stamp, which gleamed between two diamonds in her engagement ring.

Queen Mary is both a lover and a connoisseur of sapphires. She wears them often, some that are Crown Jewels, others that are family heirlooms and some that she has chosen and bought herself. Indeed, at the Wembley Exhibition her Majesty

of England rather astonished the jewel experts
from Ceylon by the careful and faultless selection
she made from a pool of sapphires they spread before her. Wishing to have thirty-four stones of almost the same size to make into a necklace, the
Queen did not relax her attention until she had
chosen them.

That is characteristic of the first lady in the
realm—complete absorption in whatever she is doing. No half and half measures, nothing haphaz-
ard. Not even in her way of wearing jewels. Sapphires being her Majesty's favourite daytime
jewel with outdoor garb, her brooch, earrings and
hatpins all match, and each is a single big sapphire
rimmed with tiny diamonds. No wonder jewellers
in quarters far removed from Bond Street tell of a
vogue for 'sapphires' whenever the Queen, on public service bent, has been down their way.

America claims to possess the biggest sapphire
in the world, one in the Morgan-Tiffany collection in the American Museum of Natural History.
This gem, known as the Star of India, weighs 543
carats and has a record of wanderings that can be
traced more or less definitely across three centuries. It is not, however, the biggest sapphire ever
discovered—one weighing 956 carats was unearthed in Burma in 1930. That also went to
America, but it has since been cut into nine pieces
as likely to be more commercially profitable than
in its original state, when it was valued at £35,000.

England's most famous sapphire is, of course, the one in the Imperial Crown. It is not a flawless gem but as it was first so worn by Charles the Second it is historically priceless. The Stuarts seem to have been rather fond of sapphires, for another such gem so named figures in Greville's Memoirs. "The King (George the Fourth) dines at Devonshire House. Lady Conyngham (the King's mistress) had on her head a sapphire which belonged to the Stuarts, and was given by Cardinal York to the King. He gave it to Princess Charlotte and when she died he desired it back, Leopold (Charlotte's husband) being informed it was a Crown jewel. This Crown jewel sparkled in the headdress of the Marchioness. I ascertained the Duke of York's sentiments on this subject the other day. He was not particularly anxious to discuss it, but he said enough to show that he has no good opinion of her."

The sapphire, more than any other precious stone unless the ruby, is associated with religious rites and ceremonies and the hierarchy of the Christian Church. A sapphire-gemmed ring is placed on the finger of the image of the Apostle in the Basilica of St. Peter in Rome every June 29, the Apostle's Feast Day. Rings set with sapphires are worn by the Cardinals of the Roman Catholic church, rings which, in olden times, were a personal gift from the Pope himself. Under the circumstances you might think that such sapphires would

be all of pretty much the same value. But not a bit
of it. There was one fifteenth century Pope who,
according to his jeweller's accounts, paid very
varying prices for the gems needed for his cardinals' rings. Presumably he had a higher personal
regard for some cardinals than for others, and the
relative measure of his esteem was indicated by
the relative value of the sapphires he bestowed.

In the Middle Ages English bishops might
choose either a sapphire or a ruby for their epis-
copal ring, but there was a definite regulation that
the gem chosen should not be engraved. Some
bishops, however, seem to have defied the regulation. Bishop Bitton of Exeter, for one, since the
ring found in his tomb in Exeter Cathedral was
set with a sapphire engraved with a hand in bene-
diction. Sapphires also, usually gemmed the gold
ring which a royal or any other highborn maiden
received when she took the veil and entered upon
a conventual life, as so many daughters of royal
and noble families did in medieval times. Such a
sapphire-set gold circlet was presented to each of
the thirteen white-robed little maidens who were
'veiled' along with Princess Mary the ten-years-
old daughter of King Edward I and Queen Elean-
or at Ambresbury in 1289. It was not a very clois-
tered nor austere existence the nun-princess led,
for she invariably joined her brothers and sisters
on festive occasions, and for her comfort her father
the King presented the Forest of Savernake for

fire for her chamber, and taxed the port of South-ampton for tuns of wine and oil for her lamp.

As a talisman the sapphire has achieved renown as great as that of any other precious stone. In the Middle Ages it was worn as a cure for ophthalmic disorders. Later it was used as a test of female virtue. Not by being offered in temptation like the jewels dangled before Margherita in *Faust*, but by attributing any change in its colour to the unfaithfulness of its wearer.

What a mercy all sapphires are not like one in South Kensington Museum which, in daylight is a deep blue but by artificial light becomes as mauve as an amethyst! In the hands of unscrupulous husbands, or rather on the fingers of their growing-old wives, such sapphires as that might bring about much marital misery. Unless, of course, the accused wife insisted on the test being made during the hours of daylight, and refused to submit to its being begun at an hour which would ensure it ending after the candles or lamps had been lighted!

A romance written round that idea was actually published in the eighteenth century. And it was suggested by the changeful sapphire now at South Kensington but then in the collection of a Count de Walchic, a Polish nobleman.

The oldest known talismanic sapphire existing in western Europe to-day once served as a clasp for the Imperial mantle covering the sacred remains of Charlemagne, the celebrated Frank ruler of Gaul, and was taken from his sarcophagus and presented to Napoleon Bonaparte when that monarch arrived at Aix-la-Chapelle just after his conquest of Germany. Mounted in gold and with a splinter of the Cross in its setting, the sapphire was supposed to give its possessor dominion over the whole world. And yet Napoleon let Josephine have it! "From that moment," say the superstitious, "the emperor's decline set in."

It would seem as if that sapphire was never meant for a Napoleon. For, when it was eventually inherited by Josephine's grandson, he, Napoleon III, promptly gave it to his wife the Empress Eugenie. And that Napoleon, like the first of his dynasty, died in exile. Now the sapphire reposes in the Cathedral of Rheims, presented thereto after the death of the Empress Eugenie by her nephew the Spanish Duke of Alba.

THE SAPPHIRE

It is mined in Australia, Burma, Ceylon, Kashmir, Siam and the U.S.A. Its name is the Greek word meaning blue. For hardness it is listed next to the diamond.

Sapphires are of many hues—pink and yellow as well as blue, but the gem mostly preferred for jewellery is the blue variety. Of this the experts consider the ideal to be an intense royal blue as to colour and velvety soft as to 'texture.' Such are the sapphires mined in Burma, Kashmir, and Siam.

Much paler and brighter is the Ceylon sapphire and it has a tinge of mauve. The Montana sapphire is usually a light, cold blue with a peculiar metallic lustre. The Australian, on the contrary is much denser and more indigo in colour, indeed, under artificial light it so darkens as to appear almost black.

What are known as Yogo sapphires come from near Yogo Gulch in Fergus County, U.S.A., and are nearly all of the true sapphire blue colour. Fergus County also produces magenta sapphires.

When looked at from the top some sapphires show a six-rayed star effect. This peculiarity is marked in the stone's 'rough' or natural state, and can be made plainer by cutting the gem en cabochon instead of with facets. Such a sapphire is known as an asteria or 'star' sapphire and is considered more valuable than the plain kind. It is mostly found in Ceylon and is mostly appreciated by American men, who wear it set in rings.

£500,000 worth of sapphires is estimated as the world's highest total production of these gems in any one year.

Chapter VI
MYSTICAL OPALS

WEMBLEY one hot day in August 1925. The Australian Pavilion at the British Empire Exhibition. A Queen, a Princess, a glint of opals. An opal miner's wife is heard saying that she would like the Queen to buy a gem from her. "Very well, I will," was her Majesty's response, "I will have this one." And so Queen Mary of England became possessed of a lovely black opal to add to her personal treasure of jewels chosen and bought by herself.

Royal predilections in the matter of precious stones can have far reaching effects, and just as King George's gift of sapphires to his only daughter on her marriage brought those gems into fashion again after long neglect, so Queen Mary's purchase of a black opal at Wembley did much to break down the ill-luck tradition which had gathered round opals whether 'white' or 'black.'

At all events the opal was the gem supreme of the following London season, and one Society bride, the Hon. Lois Sturt, daughter of Lord and Lady Alington, received a parure of black opals and diamonds as a wedding gift from her mother-in-law the Viscountess Tredegar. Moreover she went to Court in those jewels when she was presented "on her marriage," and no ornaments were more admired.

56

The opal has not always been a stone of ill-fame. Before Sir Walter Scott wrote *Anne of Geierstein* it was believed to bring good luck and to possess the combined virtues of all the other gems. Scott's story, however, put the opposite notion into people's minds. According to that romance, the Lady Hermione, Baroness of Arnheim and mother of Anne, possessed a superb opal which she wore always as a clasp to the riband binding her tresses, and which she seemed always anxious to keep from any contact with water. Indeed, lest that happen, she even refrained from crossing her forehead with Holy Water when entering church, said a malicious neighbour invited to the christening of the Baroness's daughter. The Baron, hearing this, was infuriated—

"As they passed the threshold of the chapel to the christening, the Baron dipped his finger in the font-stone. Then, as if to confute the calumnies of the malevolent Lady of Steinfeld, with an air of sportive familiarity which was rather unwarranted by time and place, he flirted on the beautiful forehead of his lady a drop or two of the moisture which remained on his own hand. The opal on which these drops had alighted shot out a brilliant spark like a falling star, and became the instant afterwards lightless and colourless as a common pebble, while the beautiful Baroness sank to the floor with a deep sigh of pain."

Nor was that all. Two hours later, on opening

e

the door of the bedchamber in which the Baroness had been deposited, "no trace of her could be discovered, unless that there was a handful of light grey ashes like such as might have been produced by burning fine paper, found on the bed where she had been laid."

So may superstitions be made and changed.Yet hardly, perhaps in Spain. There the ill-luck associated with the opal derives from a story of real life, one concerning a gem which, fifty years ago, was a love token from a Spanish monarch to his adored bride and now hangs round the neck of Our Lady of Pity in old Madrid. Death came quickly to that opal's first Bourbon wearer, and did not leave the second long alone. Then it dogged the heels of the third, he who had bestowed the gem originally and finally taken it back into his own keeping. So no wonder Queen Maria Christina regarded it as a jewel of ill omen, and when it came into her power banished it for ever beyond the reach of her kith and kin. "Let it adorn the Madonna," her Majesty is reported to have said. And there it does in the church of San Jeronimo, the very church where the last of the Bourbon kings—Alfonso XIII— took the Princess Ena of England to be his wife and queen.

Most of the world's opals are now coming from Australia and Mexico, but time was when Hungary alone supplied such gems. Those were the days when an opal in the Imperial Crown of the

Holy Roman Empire was described as of a hue that suggested "pure white snow flushed with the colour of bright ruddy wine and overcome by its radiance." That opal, moreover, was credited with shining in the night-time, and tradition said it "guarded the regal honour." But then, in Europe of the Middle Ages, the opal was widely credited with occult powers. Blonde maidens especially hankered after the gem, believing that if they could wear a necklace of opals their hair would be sure to retain its beautiful colour.

There was never an opal in the crown of England but English monarchs have worn it for all that. Queen Elizabeth often, for there was one studding a curious breast jewel of which she was very fond, a New Year's gift from one of her courtiers. And the Danish consort of King James I of England frequently flaunted opals on her fingers and wrists, judging by the numbers of rings and bracelets set with such gems which figure in the accounts rendered her Majesty by George Herriot the Court jeweller.

As for the royal ladies of France, they also appreciated opals from Hungary. Especially the Empress Josephine, who possessed one lovely opal so fiery that she named it "The Burning of Troy" and made all the ladies of her Court sick with covetousness whenever she wore it. That could scarcely be told of the Empress Eugenie for by the time she was wearing the Imperial diadem 'The Burn-

59

ing of Troy' had disappeared from the Crown Jewels of France, and the only opal she ever wore formed the body of a fly that had wings and head set with rubies, brilliants, emeralds and sapphires. Still, it must have been a valuable gem seeing that in the guise of a brooch that opal-fly fetched £320 when sold by auction at Christie's.

The biggest opal ever mined either in Hungary or anywhere else is that, four inches long and two and a half inches thick, which is in the Natural History Museum in Vienna. Rumour was pretty busy at one time about that remarkable opal, especially during Vienna's terrible financial plight following the World War. Newspapers hinted, and citizens openly expressed the fear, that this precious national possession might have to be sold to save the city from bankruptcy. Luckily when an offer of £25,000 was made by a dealer from Amsterdam, the public authorities were in a position to say "No!"

Opal mining is not nearly so dangerous an occupation as pearl-fishing. Any white man can go in for it and many do. The work is simply that of digging, and all the tools needed are a pick and a shovel. Even a woman has taken to opal-prospecting and been fairly successful. Camp life in a wild part of South Australia must have been a great change from being a shorthand-typist in a city office, but Miss M. Barrington has not regretted joining her brother in the opal workings seven hundred and fifty miles north of Adelaide. Having found enough to be going on with, she still hoped at the end of 1931 to unearth the master opal one fine day. Meanwhile she had the distinction of being the only woman among nearly two hundred men of various nationalities.

Opals are a comparatively soft substance when first mined and have to be hardened by air current set up by high speed electric fans, before they can be cut and polished. Even so they rarely become hard enough for the gem-engraver's purpose. The only engraved opal of renown is one which sixty years ago was engraved with the cameo likenesses of the then Emperor and Empress of Austria-Hungary, and the portraits took two years to do. Needless to say that opal was the sensation of the International Exhibition at Philadelphia where it was first shown.

According to ancient astrological lore the luck of human beings is influenced by the precious stones they wear, and every month of the Zodiacal year has its own special gems favourable to it. Thus the opal is the lucky jewel for all born between September 23 and October 24, but it is unfortunate for anyone whose birthday falls between June 22 and July 23, or between December 22 and January 19. The opal's Zodiacal period is termed the Dominion of Libra; its sign is a Balance or pair of scales, and all born under its influence are supposed to be endowed with extraordinary powers

of intuition and perception. The Librans are not
suited to live alone; they run best in double harn-
ess provided their partners in marriage—or busi-
ness—are not their Zodiacal antipathies, that is,
folk whose birthstone is the emerald or the ruby.

Eastern peoples regard the opal as a sacred gem
embodying the Spirit of Truth, and they believe
that its touch, if that touch be on the brow, has the
power to clear the brain and strengthen the memory. The Greeks of ancient days thought it endowed its possessor with foresight and prophetic
vision, though only if used for unselfish ends. To
the Romans of old the opal signified majesty and
power, and it is told of Nonnius, a Roman senator,
that he endured exile rather than part with an opal
Mark Anthony coveted for Cleopatra.

"The delicate colours and tenderness of an opal
remind me of a loving and beautiful child," wrote
a poet in ancient Greece. But that was before the
discovery of black opals. For a designation of the
rarer gem one must turn to a biographer in modern Britain. "It was something like Pavlova's own
mystical soul, dark and iridescent," wrote Walford
Hyden of a black opal the great Russian dancer
had given her by Australian admirers, a gem she
had set in a ring and always wore.

Masculine admiration for the black opal also
came out in another book that made a stir a few
years ago: the *Memoirs* of the late Lord Redesdale.
As a young man, and then attached to the Diplo-

matic Service, Mr A. B. Mitford as Lord Redesdale then was, dined one night with his friend Lord Overbeck who was wearing a black opal set as a tie pin. All through the meal Mr Mitford was fascinated by the fires of his friend's jewel, and could not help remarking on its extraordinary beauty. Lord Overbeck, however, rather emphasised its value as an amulet, and begged his friend to purchase one also. The upshot was that he did, whereupon Lord Overbeck remarked: "In ten days you'll get a letter, mark my words; in ten days, more or less!"

In his *Memoirs* Lord Redesdale wrote—"I went home delighted with my pretty new toy, and thought nothing more about the famous letter which I was to receive, when, on the evening of the ninth of May, exactly ten days from my purchase of the black opal, I received the following note:

10 Downing Street, Whitehall
May 9, 1874.

Dear Mr Mitford,

If you like to become Secretary to the Board of Works, I will have pleasure in appointing you.

Faithfully yours,
B. Disraeli.

"That letter changed the whole course of my life. Many years ago burglars stole the black opal."

Not every precious stone that passes through

the lapidary's hands is intended for personal wear. Eight black opals of singular beauty and great worth adorn a gold photograph frame owned by the Princess Royal. And at Windsor Castle is a globe of the world made entirely of opals, an exquisite sphere on which is poised a statue of the Winged Victory in bronze. A woman sculptor, the late Countess Feodora Gleichen was responsible for the whole design, and the sculptured figure is entirely her work, but she employed a lapidary of great taste and skill to build the opals round the globe. Alas! he was also very forgetful, and one day he left the globe in a café. Luckily, whoever walked off with it was not swift to have the lovely bauble picked to pieces for the sake of the opals it contained, else it would not, after discreet action by Scotland Yard, have been restored intact by a woman who said she had paid fifteen shillings for it at a barrow in the Caledonian Market!

THE OPAL

THIS precious substance was first mined in Hungary and as far back as early Greek and Roman times. But since the discovery of opals in Australia scarcely sixty years ago, the Hungarian mines have petered out, leaving only Mexico in rivalry with the Land of the Southern Cross. And not really that, because the Mexican fire-opal, being a translucent gem, does not compete with the opaque opals but enjoys a special favour of its own. Besides that, the Mexican opal, because of its translucency, is often facetted like the sapphire and the ruby, whereas the Australian opals are always cut in cabochon form or as beads for necklets.

The way to tell one opal from another, that is the Queensland opal from the White Cliffs variety or the Stuart's Range opal from either, is to look for its basic colour. If all the hues of the rainbow seem to glint against a strong yellow background, then the opal hails from Queensland; but if you detect a chalky whiteness behind an orange pin-fire liveliness then it is a White Cliffs opal. The characteristic of a Stuart's Range opal is a dense creamy tone offsetting the colours of the rising sun in all its glory.

Hungarian opals are easily recognised by their extremely limpid look, as of water flowing behind their splendid Harlequin hues. They are rarely seen nowadays outside museums, and the best of such places to study their beauty is the Victoria and Albert Museum at South Kensington.

The black opal is the youngest stone in the annals of Australasian gem-mining. It is unearthed at Lightning Ridge, Queensland, and when it was first offered in Europe—in the early days of the present century —dealers would not give more than £1 or £2 an ounce for it. Now it is getting near to being the costliest gem on earth. A specimen offered in London lately was valued at £10,000.

Chapter VII

THE RINGS OF KINGS AND QUEENS

ROYAL personages are very human when they fall in love, and quite as prone as less exalted mortals to cherish dearly their first gifts to each other. With all her wealth of jewels Queen Victoria to the end of her long life liked best to wear the narrow enamel ring set with a tiny diamond, which had been the Prince Consort's gift to her on his first visit to England, and also the emerald-studded snake ring he had sent her as soon as their betrothal was officially announced, when he could, therefore, with perfect propriety, supplement the bracelet containing his portrait which he had slipped on to his beloved's wrist immediately she had proposed.

A snake ring with a embellishment of emeralds! What a world of mystical meanings Queen Victoria might have read into it had she been a believer in the occult. Throughout the ages the serpent has been a symbol of Eternity and a talisman for Longevity, Health, and Vitality; while the emerald, still to Orientals, represents hopes of immortality, courage, and exalted faith.

And even in the nineteenth century an Englishwoman wrote of the emerald when worn in a ring:

66

It is a gem which hath the power to show
If plighted lovers keep their faith or no.
If faithful, it is like the Leaves of Spring,
If faithless, like those leaves when withering.

Nevertheless it is doubtful whether Queen Victoria's engagement ring meant more to her than a solemn pledge and a very precious love token. She was more a sentimentalist than a mystic. Within four days of their private betrothal she recorded in her diary that she gave Prince Albert "a ring with the ever dear 15th engraved upon it." She might have added the motto on Nerissa's ring in *The Merchant of Venice*—"Love me and leave me not." For that was what she expected of him. And he did not fail her. Nine children in less than twenty years—and then the only parting beyond the power of mortals to evade.

Queen Victoria was not, as is popularly supposed, the first English royal lady to exchange betrothal rings with her husband. Six centuries earlier, Isabella, daughter of King John, had done the same. But with this difference: that she did so without first having met the man. Ferdinand II of Germany, head of the Holy Roman Empire and King of Sicily, in making formal application for her hand through his Ambassador Pier di Vinea, presented her with a ring acclaiming her as Empress of the Holy Roman Empire, and the ring Isabella sent him in return was in token of her acceptance of his proposal.

Royal wedding rings also, have had scraps of sentiment engraved upon their burnished gold. "Dehors cet anel, pourrions avoir amour?" could be read on the marriage circlet of King Louis the Ninth of France, who in the thirteenth century was known as Saint Louis and died under the walls of Tunis while on a Crusade to the Holy Land.

"God send me weel to keepe" encircled the wedding ring of Anne of Cleves, the fourth wife of the much-marrying Henry the Eighth of England. But not for long. Within a year that ring had been returned to the donor in fear and trembling by a discarded wife who, dreading that her head might follow Anne Boleyn's to the executioner's block, consented to be known in future as Henry's adopted 'sister'!

But probably the rarest royal wedding ring of romance and renown was the one which the Stuart Pretender who styled himself "Charles III" gave his 'queen,' for engraved upon it was the couplet—

"The Crown is due to you from me
And none can love you more than me."

How characteristic of the Stuarts! They were ever good at doing things with a flourish. No other royal line had a better flair for the fine 'gesture.' Not even Napoleon Bonaparte. "To Destiny," the words Napoleon had engraved on Josephine's wedding ring sounded fine enough but they promised nothing except by implication. Still, they did yield a crown, if only for a short time, which was more than ever came to Princess Louise of Stolberg, the wife of the third Charles Stuart.

Although the posy ring has been the approved marriage circlet of many a royal bride, there have been other variants on the plain hoop of gold chosen by Mary Tudor for her marriage with Philip of spain "because maydens were so married in old tymes." Set with a diamond was the gold wedding ring of Mary of Modena, she who came to England at fifteen to marry the future James II and fled with him to France after only three years of queenly privileges.

A ruby garnished the circlet with which Henry the Sixth of England married Margaret of Anjou, the royal lady who is credited with introducing the fashion of wearing two rings on every finger except the last. Her ruby wedding ring, however, could not have been of her own choosing, seeing that it had formerly belonged to her husband's uncle the Cardinal Beaufort. As for the wedding ring which Mary Queen of Scots had from her second husband Henry Earl of Darnley, it was remarkable for being "enamelled red and bediamonded."

Some English royal weddings in by-gone days

were made memorable by the presentation of rings other than the one blessed by the priest and slipped by the bridegroom on to the bride's finger. Such rings were really wedding-favors, and their distribution to distinguished guests made as picturesque a ceremonial as the handing round of snippets of ribbon bearing the royal bride's portrait in gold, which used to characterise the nuptials of German royalties at the Prussian Court.

There was no accepted design for these wedding ring-favors—it usually depended on the personal taste of the donor. Thus when George III was married to Princess Charlotte of Mechlenburg-Strelitz, the gold presentation rings were adorned with two hearts surmounted by a crown, all in garnets, while the hoop was engraved with the legend—"George and Charlotte, united 1761," on a ground of white enamel. Thirty years later, when this royal couple's second son Frederick Duke of York espoused the eldest daughter of the King of Prussia, the gold rings distributed had the words "Soyez Heureuse" inscribed in blue enamel on the hoop, while on the bezel appeared two interlaced Y's. About the six dozen rings ordered by Queen Victoria for distribution to distinguished personages at her wedding with Prince Albert of Saxe-Coburg and Gotha there was a shade less sentiment and a shade more regality, inasmuch as they bore her likeness in profile and were inscribed "Victoria Regina."

FAMOUS RINGS AND PENDANT.

Centre : The Canning Jewel that once belonged to the Earl of Harewood,
husband of the Princess Royal.

Top left : Sixteenth century signet ring of silver engraved with a monogram.

Top right : Gold snake ring with rubies for eyes.   Said to have been the
favourite ring of King George IV.

Bottom left : Gold ring inscribed on blue enamel with two interlaced Y's.
This ring was presented by Frederick Duke of York on the occasion
of his marriage September 29th, 1791, to John Marling.

Bottom right : Portrait-ring showing on one side Anne of Austria, and on
the other her son the young Louis XIV.

By permission of the Victoria & Albert Museum.

To face page 70.]

On the whole it must have been rather an expensive way of honouring guests at a royal wedding judging by the sum—four thousand pounds sterling—which George the Fourth incurred for ring-souvenirs of his own wedding, a little bill which Parliament eventually had to pay.

This monarch, by the way, had rather a penchant for rings, but was oftenest seen wearing one in the form of a three-coil snake that had rubies for eyes. It is this ring his Majesty is wearing in the painting by Sir Thomas Lawrence which hangs in the Wallace Collection.

Rings bearing royal portraits were, of course, known to fame long before Queen Victoria's time, and were put to more momentous uses than just commemorating royal marriages. Signets such rings often were, a monarch's handy means of sealing private letters. One queen, the redoubtable Elizabeth, gave a portrait-ring to her favourite the Earl of Essex as a token and pledge of royal help in time of trouble. But the carved sardonyx cameo did not save that courtier's head when the queenly temper turned. Not because 'Gloriana' repudiated her pledge but because another woman prevented the ring reaching her.

At an earlier period of the world's history portrait-rings were worn as amulets. It is told of the Roman Emperor Hadrian, who visited Britain and had built the great wall between Newcastle and Carlisle as a protection for his dominions against the Picts and the Scots, that he always wore a ring bearing his own likeness, and that when the ring dropped from his finger the incident was taken as an omen of his coming death.

One of the most curious of royal portrait-rings still in existence, is a hoop of lead with a circular bezel finely chased in relief with the profile heads of the Spanish Emperor Charles V and his Empress. This particular monarch was anything but loved in the Netherlands, a fact the Flemish artificer of the ring ironically stressed by so making the hoop that it would serve as a whistle!

Even more historically interesting is a ring with a hoop of iron and a bezel of silver that is preserved at the Victoria and Albert Museum. Italian, of the eighteenth century, it is known as the 'Royal Family Compact Ring' because three of the four heads engraved upon it are of a king, his brother and son, all pledged, like the fourth royalty, to help a relation of theirs, the Empress Marie Theresa, in her wars to establish the Austrian Succession.

Birth not battle was commemorated by another royal family portrait-ring of historic interest, one given by the Emperor Napoleon of France to King Bernadotte of Sweden. The Swedish monarch who had once been a Marshal of France under Napoleon, and had married a sister of the Queen of Naples, one of Napoleon's sisters-in-law, tendered his congratulations on the birth of a son to his former chief, by bestowing on the French royal babe the Swedish Order of the Seraphim; and it was in return for that that Napoleon sent Bernadotte the ring. What makes this ring remarkable is that its three portraits—Napoleon, Marie Louise and the infant King of Rome—are painted on porcelain and encased as in a locket with a snap cover.

Rings were a favourite form of gift from one royalty to another in England during the reigns of the first four Georges, and it says much for their recipients that the sentimental value of such gifts was often more esteemed than their intrinsic worth. True, the brilliants set in a ring given by Queen Charlotte to George III on one of his birthdays were not undervalued by that monarch, but it is said he held the gems of less acount than the miniature they enframed—an enamel "on which were the portraits of his little ones."

Sentiment, too, inspired that monarch's mother the Dowager Princess of Wales, to give her daughter a ring bearing the words "May it bring you happiness" when she, the Princess Matilda, left England at fifteen to marry King Christian VII of Denmark. Alas! the sentiment was of little avail. That ring's recipient had about as miserable a married life as any queen could have. Goaded into conduct which led to her divorce, she was banished and died at the age of twenty-three. Not

f

many years in which to qualify for the title of 'A Queen of Tears.'

Betrothal rings, wedding rings, keeper rings, poesy rings, or portrait rings—the royal wearer's or donor's personal taste usually dictated their device and design. So it does a Coronation ring, at least to some extent and in England. For though the ruby which adorned the coronation ring intended by Richard the Second for his successors has appeared in the coronation ring of every English monarch from that time to this, its setting has not always been the same. Charles I had the historic ruby surrounded by diamonds; William IV added a sapphire.

But tradition prescribes the finger on which a coronation ring may be placed. And that is the fourth. Queen Victoria counting her little finger as her fourth, had her masculine predecessor's ring altered to fit her slenderer proportions. But to what idle purpose! For, lo! and behold, at her coronation the Archbishop of Canterbury, instead of slipping the ring on her Majesty's little finger thrust it on to her next, much to the Queen's hurt and discomfort. So much so, that to get the ring off at the end of the ceremony in order that it might be packed away with the rest of the royal regalia, there had to be much bathing of the royal finger in iced water in the privacy of the royal retiring room.

Not the wrong finger but the wrong ring made

74

jewel history at another English coronation. For the ruby ring which Queen Mary II had enlarged to wear when she and William were jointly crowned in Westminster Abbey was, by mistake, put on the King's finger, much to the consternation of the Queen. For it had been William's first gift to her, and its transference to the donor no doubt seemed a happening of ill-omen. Mary did, however, get the ring back into her own keeping, and thenceforth it was carefully kept under lock and key as something too precious to wear.

Being a personal possession that ruby ring of the Dutch William's English wife never became a Crown Jewel, but on Mary's death was given as a memento to William Bentinck, first Earl of Portland. And now it abides down in the depths of Sherwood Forest, treasured by the Duke of Portland behind the massive seventeenth century portals of Welbeck Abbey.

No gems gleamed in the rings of kings and queens of Anglo-Saxon times. Yet royal finger circlets thenadays did not lack beauty, as can be seen by those of nielloed gold, bearing the names of King Ethelwulf and Queen Ethelswith, which are in the British Museum.

The Pope's Investiture ring is also gemless, but not for the same reason—there were plenty of precious stones and skilled lapidaries in Rome when that historic golden circlet first came into usage about the middle of the thirteenth century.

The interest of the Papal ring lies in the engraved bezel with its representation of St. Peter in a boat casting a net into the sea, a device which accounts for the circlet's popular name—The Ring of the Fisherman.

Once upon a time the Ring of the Fisherman was but the private seal of Roman Pontiffs, and used mainly for their letters. For nearly four centuries now it has been officially associated with the election of each new Pope, being placed on his finger by the Cardinal Chamberlain who at the same time enquires what name he will take. The Pope having formally replied, back goes the golden circlet to the goldsmith to have the chosen name engraved just above St. Peter's head.

THE FINGER RING

OUT OF Egypt has come the oldest royal ring extant, that worn by Cheops, the Pharaoh who built the Great Pyramid three thousand years B.C. It is of gold engraved with hieroglyphics.

Ancient Egyptian rings were not always of metal—gold, silver or bronze—but sometimes of faience. One such ring dating back to 2,500 years B.C. was bequeathed to the nation by Sir Augustus Franks. It is of green faience and has a cartouche two inches long bearing the legend "Amen Ra, Lord of the Thrones of the World."

Married women in Egypt used to wear rings as amulets to ensure a happy and easy childbirth. A favourite design in such amulet rings had the bezel shaped like a chapel in which was a tiny bust of the goddess Isis-Hathor.

The ancient Greeks were great on rings engraved with female figures—not always those of goddesses. Several Greek rings dating four or five centuries B.C. are embellished with female figures represented in such everyday attitudes as standing by a tripod, or tying their sandals, even as playing knucklebones!

Roman rings, on the contrary, were often adorned with representations of animals, serpents and famous warriors. And besides being of gold, silver, bronze, or the lesser metals like lead and iron, Roman rings were made of jet and amber, red earthenware, white cornelian and lapis lazuli.

To the ancient Romans we owe the betrothal or engagement ring. With them, however, its presentation was not a private affair between lovers, but a formal ceremony on the occasion when the father or guardian of the future bride pledged his word on her behalf.

From the Romans of a later era we get the love ring as distinct from the betrothal ring. In its oldest form the love ring represents two clasped hands, whence its name "fede," derived from the Italian phrase "Mani in fede," literally "Hands in Faith."

In England of the Middle Ages the wedding ring was placed on the bride's right hand. The change to the left came about in the sixteenth century and was prescribed by the rubric in the Sarum Manual. English Catholics, however, stuck to the right hand custom up to the middle of the eighteenth century. During the reign of the first two Georges it became the custom for the bride to transfer her wedding ring to her thumb after the ceremony, and it is represented so worn in portraits of the period.

In the Orthodox Church it is customary for the bridegroom to give the bride a gold ring and to receive a silver ring from the bride. Both rings are worn on the right hand.

At a Jewish wedding the bridegroom places the ring on the middle finger of the bride's right hand. But it is only worn during the service—not afterwards. That is because of its unwieldly size. Many Jewish wedding rings represent a synagogue or Solomon's Temple, and usually bear some sort of motto—often "Good Luck" in Hebrew lettering. Hebrew betrothal rings are equally cumbersome and elaborate. One bequeathed to the nation by Baron Ferdinand Rothschild is in the form of a gold cylinder bearing a pierced plate engraved with the Creation, the Fall, and the expulsion of Adam and Eve from Eden.

Add royal rings to magical rings, and then betrothal rings to marriage rings, and still the sum total of ring species will not be complete without taking into account signet rings and religious rings, commemoration rings and mourning rings as well

as the official rings of bishops and the lesser digni-
taries of the Church. Even medieval abbesses wore
rings by virtue of their office, though the practice
was prohibited by Pope Gregory XIII in the sixteenth century.

Chapter VIII
TURQUOISES FOR A ROYAL
DUCHESS

IF YOU would know why H.R.H. the Duchess of York always wears a parure of turquoises and diamonds whenever, as the third lady of the realm, she is nearby the King and Queen during a Royal Court at Buckingham Palace, it is because of King George's profound belief that a lovely woman is made lovelier by wearing jewels that match her eyes. And so that it might be thus with his son's bride, his Majesty gave her Persian turquoises as a wedding gift. Tiara, necklace, earrings and corsage brooch—they intensify the intense blue of the royal wearer's eyes and heighten the darkness of her dark brown hair.

As with the oldtime kings of Burma and the rubies mined in thier kingdom, the Shahs of Persia have always had royal rights in the turquoise mines of Kishapur, and even to this day the finest stones are sent to the Persian monarch for his inspection —and retention if he so desires. That is why the largest turquoise in the world—a gem four inches long—abides in the Treasure Room of the Royal Palace at Teheran.

Why also, in that Treasure Room behind the locked door with the thrice-sealed locks, is one of the most curious examples of gem work ever fashioned, a globe showing the different countries of the world defined by various precious stones, Persia being inlaid with turquoises, and the seven seas with emeralds. Twenty years ago that globe was valued at £947,000.

In Persia the turquoise is regarded as the most powerful of all amulets against the influence of the Evil Eye, so one is early hung round a baby's neck, especially a boy-baby's. For Persian parents esteem sons above daughters. "He that hath no son hath no light in his eyes" runs an old saying; and it is looked upon as a disgrace if a man has no heir to carry on his name.

Perhaps it is because Persian women were for centuries held of little account as compared with Persian men, that they rarely wore this gem up to a generation or two ago, whereas most men flaunted it habitually, usually in a ring. Or was man's monopoly of the turquoise due to his greater need of its supposed protective powers? Certainly "the open road and the bright eyes of danger" has been the masculine lot in Persia from time immemorial. And still is, more or less in that land of desert plains, mountain passes, and a scarcity of railways.

What wonder, then, that a gem credited with the power to guard its wearer from injury should he fall when walking or riding, is always in the keeping of the man of the family? It had, however, to be worn either on the index finger or the little finger for its spell to be potent.

As a matter of fact Persian women have not

gone entirely without turquoises, but such as they have had were generally 'seed' turquoises of little value and only considered fit to ornament the tiny gold filigree boxes containing quotations from the Koran, which Persian women wear strapped to their arms as a charm against sterility.

Still, even seed turquoises can be as useful as the bigger and costlier gems worn by the men, when it comes to obeying the behest about the new moon, a behest which says that whoever looked upon a turquoise immediately after looking at the new moon the first night it was visible, was destined to be prosperous.

One of the oldest beliefs about the turquoise is that which credits the gem with a benign influence upon horses. Attached to bridle or girth it would keep a horse from stumbling in stony places, and from suffering ill effects after drinking cold water when overheated by exertion. Indeed the turquoise is to the Persian horse what 'brasses' used to be to its English counterpart—an amulet to safeguard it against evil happenings. And not only in Persia. England of the late seventeenth century adopted the Persian idea.

Mistress John Lane, who helped Charles II to safety during his flight after the battle of Worcester by having him ride pillion behind her disguised as a serving-man, was in the habit of using a turquoise studded riding whip. History does not tell whether she did so from faith or from vanity.

But at any rate though her horse cast a shoe on that historic journey it did not unseat the two riders.

Here in the West during the Middle Ages, when belief in astrology was widespread, the turquoise was considered the lucky gem for all born between April 21 and May 22. Not that a woman whose birthday fell in that Zodiacal month would wear no other gems—she just always took care to have a turquoise about her person in order to ensure prosperity in love. There is a legend that Catherine de Medicis who ruled as Regent in France in the sixteenth century, was so determined not to miss any of the good luck that was going in connection with the precious stones dedicated to the various months of the Zodiacal year, that she had a girdle gemmed with the whole twelve!

That later royalties deemed the turquoise a jewel of felicity is indicated by the frequency with which it appeared in the personal ornaments made for Anne, consort of James the First of England by George Herriot the Court Jeweller. One item reads—"A little pendant diamond hung at the heart of a turquoise." The great Napoleon, too, when a young man, evidently favoured the turquoise in affairs of the heart for the first ring he gave Josephine was a narrow gold circlet gemmed with six tiny turquoises, a relic now among the French national treasures at the Louvre.

What is said to be one of the finest turquoises ever owned and worn by a Persian monarch, is not now in Persia but in Russia as part of the relics of bygone Imperial splendour, and it is remarkable because its two inches of blue hydrated aluminium phosphate are inscribed with a text from the Koran lettered in gold. Time was when the rulers of Persia—and their queens—gratified their egotism by wearing turquoises engraved with their own portraits. But this was put a stop to round about the seventh century by the priesthood declaring it impious as contrary to the precept of the Koran forbidding the reproduction of the likeness of any living thing. However, rather than antagonise the lapidaries word went forth that the faithful would find gems engraved with pious phrases very efficacious as amulets, and thenceforth the signet rings of the Persians were so engraved.

After Persia, Tibet is the country in Asia where turquoises are most assiduously collected—but by women, not men. Probably no other men or women in the world wear as many turquoises and so continuously as do the Tibetan women. For they stud their head-dress with them, and this head-dress not only literally covers the head but spreads over the shoulders as well. Even a queen—there is a queen in Tibet, the wife of the deposed King of Ladakh—wears this kind of head-dress and displays her turquoises in the self-same way. Being also comparatively poor she regards turquoises much as the less exalted Tibetan women do, that is as her banking account. And like them she looks upon the turquoise as a barometer of health, for when its wearer is ill the stone becomes dull.

To the Indians of New Mexico the turquoise is a sacred stone, and they have no faith in any medicine-man who does not possess such a gem. Their name for turquoise is *duklig* which signifies either a blue or green stone. They often affix a turquoise to their hunting weapons, believing that then the shot will go straight to the mark.

Perhaps it is as well that nowadays among white people in the western hemisphere, jewel superstitions have ceased to be of much importance. It leaves a woman freer to be swayed by sentiment, colour and craftsmanship in choosing her personal ornaments. And it is less restricting to would-be donors if there is no need to consider whether a recipient might be affronted or affrighted by the bestowal of some particular gem. Royalties especially, would be tied in the giving and receiving of jewels were Zodiacal or astrological lore allowed to rule the matter. Better be eclectic where precious stones are concerned, and trust to one cancelling the other out when it comes to a question of evil influences or good. Some people commented adversely on the lack of aquamarines among the ex-Queen of Spain's jewels at the time of her marriage, the aquamarine being her birthstone according to the Zodiacal calendar. Others rejoiced that she did not lack turquoises—exquisite oblong

stones linked with diamonds in the form of a necklace given her by her uncle and aunt the then
Princess of Wales—afterwards King Edward and
Queen Alexandra. Yet all the same the turquoises
did not save from death the horses drawing the
State coach on that disastrous royal wedding day.
And though King Alfonso later crammed his wife's
jewel casket with aquamarines, there came a time
when he and she had to forgo their royal preroga-
tives and flee the country where they had sat en-
throned.

If, as it seems, turquoises did not appeal to Russian royalties as strongly as did other coloured
gems, they nevertheless figured very effectively
in some of the diadems worn by the Grand Duch-
esses on occasions of Imperial splendour at the
Winter Palace. That most fascinating publication
of modern times, the Illustrated Catalogue of the
Russian Imperial Treasure issued by the Soviet
Government in four languages—English, French
and German as well as Russian—shows one very
lovely turquoise diadem that has the blue stones
framed in strips of gold. And its curving circlets of
silver-set diamonds inside which the turquoises
are poised, have little golden galleries and leaves
in between.

That blend of blue and gold in the personal
ornament of a royal lady's choosing, how it reveals
the Russian craving for colour! Or did in the days
when golden cupolas, sacred ikons and the gor-

(Vandyk).

QUEEN ENA OF SPAIN WEARING HER DIADEM AND PENDANT OF
AQUAMARINES AND DIAMONDS.

To face page 86.]

geous vestments of a bearded priesthood were the memories longest visualised by English visitors to the land of the Romanoffs. Not that the colour urge is peculiar to Russians. In varying degrees it characterises other dwellers in far northern latitudes where winter lingers long and snow abounds. The young Crown Princess of Norway has exemplified this, though perhaps unconsciously. Her bridal jewels were pearls and diamonds. But when her husband wished to give her more jewels in commemoration of the birth of their first child, her Royal Highness chose turquoises. Diamonds rim the blue gems but they are small in comparison with the large pear-shaped Persian turquoises pendant from round ones nearly as big, which compose the Crown Princess's Memorial necklace. And very lovely the royal mother looked wearing it at the christening of her baby daughter the Princess Ragnhild in the palace chapel at Oslo.

Turquoises from Persia! I know a Cotswold garden that owes its wonderful colour scheme to them. Blue flowers flank its greensward alleys, blue flowers grow in the crevices of its flagged paths. A stone fountain sprays into a basin lined with tiny tiles of turquoise glaze. The waters of a large pool shine turquoise in the sunlight, an effect cleverly gained by encasing them in cement enamelled blue.

And when the woman whose joy this garden is, walks in her perfumed pleasaunce as the heat of a brilliant summer day cools at the touch of evening zephyrs, she does so with turquoises clasping her throat. Ah! that throat! Once upon a time the world raved about it. That was in pre-war days when Mary Anderson thrilled theatre-goers on both sides of the Atlantic with her portrayal of a statue come to life. Now, in the retirement of a happy marriage 'Galatea' is famed for the glories of the wonderful blue garden she has made and the beauty of the jewels she wears.

THE TURQUOISE

IT IS mined in both the Old World and the New. Persia produces the finest, but some very lovely specimens come from the U.S.A.—Arizona, California and Nevada.

New Mexico also yields turquoises and thence came those that are among the old Crown Jewels of Spain, mute reminders of Spanish conquest in Central America three hundred years ago.

Mexican turquoises are mined as primitively now as then. And that is with the native substitute for dynamite, namely by heating with huge fires the rock in which the turquoise matrix is embedded and then cooling it sharply with cataracts of cold water, a process that causes the rock to split.

Turquoises are not called turquoises in Persia. They never were; it is not a Persian word but one coined in Europe because the gem was first intro-

CROWN PRINCESS OF NORWAY WEARING THE NECKLACE OF TURQUOISES
AND DIAMONDS, WHICH WAS HER HUSBAND'S GIFT ON THE BIRTH OF
THEIR FIRST DAUGHTER, THE PRINCESS RAGNILD.

To face page 88.]

duced to the West by way of Turkey. The name for the stone in Persia is "Firunza" meaning "Victory." And a victory it literally represents when it has been wrested from rock by no other tool than a hand chisel.

The famous Persian turquoise mines are at Kishapur in the north-east corner of the province of Khorassan near Omar Khayyam's birthplace, and they are worked by men whose broad flat faces and high cheek bones proclaim a Mogul ancestry. And like the diamond diggers of South Africa the turquoise miners of Persia are searched when their day's work is done, though that does not prevent many of the best stones being concealed and illicitly sold.

The typical colour of a turquoise is a delicate sky blue, but the present fashion decrees that the deeper the blue the finer the gem. Both time and sunlight affect a turquoise, causing it to lose some of its blueness and acquire a green tinge. Which explains why antique turquoises are sometimes more green than blue.

Being opaque, a turquoise is always cut en cabochon and never facetted.

Chapter IX

AN EMPRESS WHO WORE CORAL

MUCH as she loved her jewelled diadems and doted on her girdles set with pearls, the Empress Josephine of France had a liking for coral. En cabochon it rimmed several of those hair ornaments known as "frontlets" which she wore so often on occasions that did not call for ceremonious attire.

Coral was, indeed, rather a cult at the Court of Napoleon I. The Emperor's favourite sister, the Princess Pauline Borghese, she who had married an Italian nobleman as her second husband and finding Society in Rome deadly dull had returned to Paris and the gaieties of the Tuileries, did as much as the Empress to make coral the fashion. Perhaps more so, for she allied it with diamonds, greatly to the coral's glorification and her own aggrandisement. In one year alone and at one particular jeweller's the Princess Pauline spent 250,000 francs on personal ornaments and of that sum 31,000 francs went in a set of corals and diamonds.

Not that there wasn't some excuse for such lavish expenditure. Napoleon expected all his family to keep up a style of living that would make his Court and Paris Society superior to any in Europe. And on Pauline especially did he depend greatly for social help during the interval that elapsed between his divorcement of Josephine and his marriage with the Austrian Archduchess Marie Louise. Foreign royalties had to be impressed both before and on their arrival in France for the Imperial nuptials. Pauline could hardly be expected to play hostess for an Emperor unless superbly bejewelled. Hence the diamonds rimming her corals.

That Napoleon's second wife should also take to wearing coral rather suggests that the Emperor deliberately encouraged the fashion for political reasons, the Italians, then as now, being noted for the coral they worked and exported. At all events Napoleon gave the mother of his son a girdle whereon the Imperial bees were encrusted in pearls and coral. And that ornament went with Marie Louise when, on Napoleon's banishment, she fled back to her native land. It remained with her, too, longer than some of the jewels carried away in like circumstances, so she was able to bequeath it by will to her English friend Lady Burgersh.

The social eminence of coral in France during the thirty years following the eclipse of the First Empire was nothing to speak of, and it seems to have needed the marriage of the Duc d'Aumale with a Princess of the Two Sicilies to make it the mode again. The new Duchess had quite a lot of coral ornaments in her corbeille de mariage, and the frequency with which she appeared in public wearing them, soon caused coral to be the rage for

daytime jewellery. Coral necklaces encircled col-
umn-like throats, broad bands of coral clasped
dimpled wrists, and brooches of coral in all shapes
and sizes pinned lace berthes above plump bosoms.

And that not in France only. The fashion spread
to England and to Holland. True, it never seems
to have enjoyed royal favour in England, probably because Queen Victoria was notoriously
partial to precious stones, especially diamonds.
But outside Court circles coral ornaments were
much worn. And very charming they could be,
judging by specimens now preserved in various
national collections. Our Victorian ancestors may
have been too prone to prefer the massive alike in
furniture, pictures and personal ornaments, but at
least they appreciated fine craftsmanship, as the
carved coral jewellery of their fancy clearly tells.

So it was with their contemporaries across the
North Sea in Holland. Dutch people have an even
greater reputation than the English for liking
things solid, but they, too, bought and wore some
of the loveliest carved coral ornaments that ever
came out of Italy. One of the present-day attrac-
tions of Amsterdam to feminine visitors is the
Suasso collection of nineteenth century jewelry
with its wonderful assortment of coral bracelets,
brooches, necklaces and earrings. Coral had, of
course, been worn by Dutch women before the
nineteenth century but usually as beads and by
farmers' wives and daughters. What makes the

coral jewelry in the Suasso collection so fascinating is that it once belonged to Dutch dames of high degree, and yet is akin in character to the personal ornaments of like substance fashionable in France during the Second Republic.

The wearing of coral during the early nineteenth century whether by English, French, or Dutch women was mostly a matter of fashion, but in England of the Middle Ages coral was coveted for the magical and medicinal virtues ascribed to it. And a favourite way of carrying it about was in the form of a rosary suspended from the girdle or else wound round the wrist as a bracelet. One of the earliest inventories extant, that of the personal possessions of Margaret and Alianore de Bohun, daughters of the Earl of Hereford and Essex who was slain at the battle of Boroughbridge in 1321, mentions a rosary of coral beads with gilded gaudee (the larger beads). It also mentions three branches of coral, though it does not particularise as to whether those coral branches were engraved or plain. Medieval preference was, on the whole, for engraved coral, as heightening its efficacy as an amulet.

Coral engraved with a serpent or a gorgon's head was believed to afford protection against all enemies and wounds; if combined with lodestone to form a necklace, a woman would find it a help to easy childbirth. Much the same superstitious faith is at the root of the custom of giving a string of coral beads as christening present to a girl-baby, and a rattle of silver bells on a coral stem to a boy-baby, a practice more prevalent in Victorian times than ours. Not that boy-babies have never been adorned with strings of coral. It is told of King Louis the Thirteenth of France that as a babe he early had a coral necklace fastened round his neck and a little turquoise ring put upon his finger.

All the best coral used by jewellers of the western world has come from the Mediterranean sea, and the fishing rights for it thereabouts have see-sawed through the centuries between Italy and France. Now France controls the coral fisheries along that part of Mediterranean-African coast where her colonies lie; Italy makes good with what she gets from roundabout her island possessions.

Every year sees the coral fishers of Santa Margherita on the Gulf of Spezia sail away to the coral reefs that lie hidden beneath the sunlit waters of the Tyrrhenian Sea off Sardinia; October brings them back tired out to the point of exhaustion.

Dredging for coral is heavy work. A weighty wooden cross is the chief apparatus, and to this stout nets are attached and sunk fathoms deep by means of a gigantic stone. Owing to these tremendous weights the boats rock a good deal, so that not infrequently even the most hardened fishers have bouts of sea-sickness.

And soft and warm as summer can be afloat

these southern waters, the men of the coral fleet are worn out by the end of the season, for their work has to be carried on day and night with but short intervals for rest and sleep. After the coral has been hauled aboard, it has to be roughly cleansed and packed in boxes for despatch mainly to Genoa and Naples. These two cities have almost a monopoly of working-up coral: there is a whole Neapolitan suburb which does nothing but cut and polish and carve and string it.

Not all coral is pink or red when fished up from the sea. Some of it is black, though it will gleam crimson after a three-days' bath in peroxide. Which is why coral cargoes are auctioned in harbour, and why coral merchants will give as much as £10 per ounce for coral that needs no such revivifying.

Except for babies' rattles, the naturally nobbly surface of coral is little wanted by the craftsmen who mount the substance into articles of bijouterie for the European market, so it is got rid of by means of a small grindstone dipped in water. To see the girls is to realise what a highly skilled job it is, and why only the most experienced 'hands' are entrusted with it.

The coral workers of Italy are nearly all girls. Theirs is the task of boring, planing, and polishing this curious product of submarine insects. Men, usually, are engaged to do the cutting, a process demanding judgment as well as deftness,

95

since a seemingly poor piece may contain well-shaped fragments, and not to detect them would be as wasteful as spoiling a fine piece by clumsy cutting. But even this job has been entrusted to women; one employer there used to be in Leghorn who would have none other than female "hands" in his works. And he housed them, too, with patrician spaciousness, in a mansion set in a smiling garden not far from the Villa Valsovano, on the roof of which Shelley wrote most of the *Cenci*.

As might be expected of a country where coral is a means of livelihood for many folk, Italy can show some curious uses to which "peau d'ange," as the Neapolitans call coral, has been put. At Loreto on the shores of the Adriatic, a place famous for the miraculous black Madonna, there is a picture of the Holy House— the cot of black bricks in which this statue is supposed to have been brought from the East—entirely outlined on white satin with a multitude of coral necklaces. It is a devotee's gift of long ago, a thank offering for health restored, just as is a large pearl bearing an impression of a human hand, which ranks among the jewels of the Madonna on the day of the Great Festa every December.

If, as is sometimes hinted at, the coral fisheries of the Mediterranean are gradually becoming unproductive, it is quite possible that Europe will have to depend on the Orient for all of this sub-

stance the women of the West demand. Then,
how Japan would rejoice! For she possesses an island in her southern waters that is said to be literally
fringed with coral reefs whence the yield is prolific.
Much of it, too, is very choice, though there has
never yet been a replica of the wonderful branch
which makes the perfect tree of rose-pink coral
now among the Japanese Imperial treasures and
said to be worth five thousand pounds.

Still, what Japan's coral may lack in beauty of
form, Japan's craftsmen make up for by their artistry. The little animals they carve out of coral are
marvels of anatomical accuracy and characterised
by individual traits that go beyond the natural
movements and attitudes of each particular species. Of such eastern artistry there are keen connoisseurs in the western world, and never any lack
of bidders when such curios are among the mer-
chandise put up for auction at the Cutler street
warehouse of the Port of London Authority.

Once upon a time Japan did a profitable trade
with China in coral for Mandarins' buttons, but
since Mandarins went the way of the Monarchy,
coral of high-grade quality has not been greatly
wanted in the Land of the Lion and the Sun. Coral
of one kind or another is, however, always in
steady demand throughout India and among the
more or less civilised peoples of Central Asia. One
ex-king, the deposed Rajah of Ladakh in Tibet,
still dons a crown of corals with earrings to match,

whenever he wishes to impress callers from England or the United States of America.

Here in the West the royal wearers of coral are mostly juveniles, though H.R.H. the Duchess of York numbers a chaplet of corals among her treasured trinkets. It has a romantic history, too, being a gift she accepted from a dancing-girl on one of the isles of the South Pacific during her trip to Australia with the Duke in 1926. Perhaps it appealed as a mystical link with home. For, on the eve of her departure for the Antipodes, the Duchess had clasped a string of coral beads—her own babyhood's relic—round the neck of her eight-months-old daughter the little Princess Elizabeth. With the dusky equatorial maiden's gift in her fingers Her Royal Highness had another vivid reminder, besides the photographs in her cabin, of the golden-crested babe she had had to leave behind in England.

CORAL

IT is a carbonate of lime secreted from sea water and deposited in the tissues of tiny animals working in countless myriads raising coral reefs and islands. Coral takes ten years to grow, which explains why many State-owned reefs are divided into ten portions and only one portion worked annually.

Coral was one of the earliest substances used for personal ornaments. Coral beads have been found during excavations on the site of an Assyrian king's palace at Nineveh dating from the first half of the third millennium B.C.

The ancient Greeks used to bind coral to the masthead of their sea-going vessels with the skin of a seal, to avert winds and tempests. They also believed that coral would preserve them from defeat in battle. So did the Gauls, and to that end they ornamented their weapons of war and helmets with it.

Among the ancient Romans coral was chiefly worn by children, and they had branches of it hung round their necks to preserve them from danger. Present-day Italian peasant women wear coral as a cure for sterility.

The East has always been the best market for coral, India especially, for there it is highly esteemed as a substance endowed with mysterious sacred properties. That is why rosaries of coral are much sought after by rich Buddhists and Muslims and why, there being one hundred and eight beads in a Muslim rosary as compared with the Roman Catholic rosary's fifty-four, the Oriental demand for coral is perpetually bigger than the European.

Chapter X
EARRINGS OF ROYAL FANCY

Q. When are earrings not earrings?
A. When they are Queen Elizabeth's and worn by
  King Edward.

NO—there is no catch in the conundrum. King
Edward the Seventh once did wear Queen Elizabeth's earrings. It was at his coronation. But they
did not dangle from his ears, they swung high up
in the arches of the Imperial crown, and by his
Majesty's express command had not been altered
in the slightest. The two pear-shaped pearls each
set atop with a small diamond, were complete
with the ear-hooks just as they had been made for
the ears of the Virgin Queen at her coronation.

For centuries those royal earrings had been
numbered among the disused Crown jewels. King
Edward's happy fancy to have them, intact, adorn
his coronation diadem, gave to his crowning a
touch of romance that makes it unique in history.
Indeed the sixteenth century queen's earrings
nearly took the shine out of those worn by the
twentieth century Queen Alexandra, big diamond
solitaires as those were.

Still, her Majesty wore the historic Koh-i-Nor
in her all-diamond crown, and that probably was
romance and renown enough for any queen-consort.

Queen Mary has always been fond of earrings, a taste she inherited from her mother the Duchess of Teck, who wore such ornaments habitually, believing they preserved the eyesight. Which was probably why she had her daughter's ears pierced early. 'Princess May' began to wear earrings while she was still in the schoolroom—just plain gold circlets that gave place to more elaborate ones when she put up her hair. One special pair of which she was very fond were jasper cameos, their narrow gold rims spaced by tiny gold knobs.

Not until she was betrothed did her Majesty wear diamonds at her ears, and then only small ones. Married, and a throne in prospect, her jewels gradually became handsomer and more numerous, thanks to Queen Victoria, who had set the pace by giving the young bride a diamond tiara to supplement the diamond riviere from the bridegroom's parents.

Now, on occasions, Queen Mary wears diamonds at her ears as big as any woman could desire. And besides her solitaires—of pearls as well as diamonds —her Majesty has earrings of diamonds framing other gems, maybe a pearl, a sapphire or an emerald—as her various diadems and necklaces necessitate to achieve ensemble perfection.

But the earrings of royal fancy most novel in recent years are in the form of portrait-medallions of Princess Elizabeth and Princess Margaret Rose, rimmed squarely in aquamarines. And what a stir

they made when first her Majesty appeared wearing them! Immediately the hopes of jewellers
everywhere soared high. They surmised, and
rightly so, that ladies of lesser rank would be eager
to exalt their own best-beloved in the same pretty
way.

Long pendant earrings have never appealed to
Queen Mary though when Duchess of York she
sometimes wore them on occasions of fancy dress.
One such occasion was the Duchess of Devonshire's famous historic costume ball, said to be the
most brilliant event of the Diamond Jubilee season. The royal earrings then were long strands of
diamonds and pearls, as was historically demanded
for an impersonation of a Princess in the suite of
Margaret de Valois.

Luckily those earrings were not as weighty as
some which dangled from other Royal ears on
another occasion when motley was the only wear.
It is told of the last Tzarina of Russia that at a costume ball she and the Tzar gave at the Hermitage
Palace, St. Petersburg, the earrings to complete
her attire as a byegone empress were so heavy that
they had to be fastened round her ears with gold
wires. Her head-dress, too, was frightfully weighty, so much so that to her dismay at supper she
found she could not bend her head to eat!

Weight seems, indeed, to have been inseparable
from feminine ornaments in olden times. Woman
then had no choice but to suffer to be beautiful.

Nowadays she would rebel, though perhaps not as naively as did the Grand Duchess Marie of Russia about twenty years ago.

Being a niece of the Tzar, tradition decreed that at her marriage the Grand Duchess should wear certain Crown jewels, among them a pair of heavy diamond earrings shaped like, and as big as, cherries.

All through the long trying ceremony the eighteen-years-old bride endured the weight of those earrings, but at the bridal banquet in the evening they had come to hurt her so intolerably that she took them off and hung them on the edge of the glass of water in front of her, much to the Tzar's amusement.

In the light of subsequent events that gesture of ridding herself of something too painful to be borne, was almost prophetic. Within a few years she had got her marriage annulled and was back again in the land of her birth.

Medallion earrings are no new thing in Royal jewel caskets, but those of other queens never symbolised such tender sentiments as Queen Mary's do. Perhaps those of the Tudor Elizabeth could hardly be expected to, she being a spinster, though she was fond enough of children, and showed almost maternal tenderness when brought in contact with the children of her nobles. The particular earrings of Queen Elizabeth's which historians stress, were circular rubies framed en medallion with pearls and finished with long pear-shaped pendants.

Probably the most famous medallion earrings of Royal choice were those made in the eighteenth century for the Empress Marie Theresa of Austria. They were of gold inset with medallions of the Crown of Hungary rimmed with pearls, and they matched a necklace, a bracelet and a hair-comb. Of that parure its Royal owner was immensely proud, and several Court painters have portrayed her wearing it.

Such ornaments, however, did not please a later and more temperamental Empress, Elizabeth wife of Francis Joseph, and she would never wear them. But they were accounted among the most precious of the Austrian Crown Jewels, and would now be worth a fortune to the ex-Empress Zita had they not been stolen mid the throes of the Revolution that sent her into exile.

Although not Crown jewels, a pair of earrings presented to the bride of the tragic-fated Crown Prince Rudolph of Austria created a sensation almost as great as if they had had a hectic history behind them. For they were in the form of gold rosettes enamelled with black negro heads, complete with white eyes and feather ornaments, a design that subtly—or ironically—commemorated the conquest of the Congo by the bride's father King Leopold II of Belgium. The earrings matched a necklace whereon the black enamelled negro heads numbered sixty, each set off with a large ruby. Fiume, then in Austrian and not Italian territory as now, sent the Princess Stephanie this decidedly original suite of jewellery.

Since Queen Ena of Spain became a queen without a throne, popular interest in her jewels has had little to feed upon. But before Fate sent her into exile, her Spanish Majesty's every appearance in public could be counted on to give joy to lovers of beautiful gems. For she was never without some at her ears or round her throat, and there were occasions, such as the Easter ceremonies at Court, when she literally blazed with jewels from head to heel. Tradition prescribed that she should, and the Church gave her encouragement. Immense aquamarines and diamonds have swung from Queen Ena's ears and scintillated in her diadem as she has knelt to wash the beggar's feet in the Palace chapel on Maundy Thursday. Earrings equally ravishing, but of pearls and diamonds, have matched the jewelled head-dress she has worn at High Mass on Easter Sunday. And because the attendant company of lesser royalties, Court ladies and Grandees has been apparelled and bejewelled with scarcely less splendour, the populace lining the palace corridors to watch the royal procession pass from the private apartments to the chapel, never lacked for thrills.

Nor for data as to the type of earrings favoured in Court circles, a little matter about which the

h 105

Spanish people were at one time rather touchy. For when King Alfonso's bride-elect had arrived in Spain wearing 'stud' earrings it was feared she would disdain the true Spanish type, long and swinging. The fears, however, were groundless. Her Majesty soon accepted a set of regional jewelry from the province of Salamanca and what is more, was photographed wearing it—high gilded comb, yards of gilt beads, long gold cross earrings and all. Better still, she took to wearing long jewelled earrings with her Court dresses. So if the Salamancans claim that they had much to do with the conversion of the English-born queen to a Spanish habit in earrings, who shall say them nay?

Among the younger generation of European royalties it is the Crown Princess of Italy who shows the most pronounced liking for long earrings. And did, even before her marriage, although her mother, Queen Elizabeth of the Belgians, rarely wears earrings of any kind. An Egyptian costume ball in Brussels when she was but nineteen, was the Princess's initiation into the fascination of ear ornaments. Attired as a royal lady of the Tut-ankh-Amen period, Her Royal Highness went to that ball wearing jewellery of the correct type for such an impersonation, as well she might, seeing that her mother had been over in Egypt for the formal opening of the great Pharaoh's burial shrine and had seen the wonderful treasure of gold and bead ornaments the Tut-ankh-Amen tomb had yielded. So armlets and anklets, bracelets and head filet, together with the characteristically Egyptian collar of tubular beads threaded in three tiers, went to transform the Belgian King's daughter into the semblance of an Egyptian princess who lived four thousand years ago. They did more—they effected a change in her personality. At least, she who had never before displayed any special interest in Fashion, thenceforth developed an amazing chic, and with it a passion for wearing earrings.

Indeed, by the time she was betrothed, H.R.H. possessed so many pairs of earrings that her fiancé is reported to have laughingly said she must have heard of an old Piedmontese custom and determined to evade it. For in Piedmont, the province whence the Italian heir-apparent takes one of his titles, a pair of earrings, instead of a finger ring, used to be a man's first gift to the maiden he was about to marry, and etiquette demanded he should insert the earrings himself. But as etiquette also demanded that the holes for the earrings should be made by the gold wires of the betrothal earrings, the piercing took place to the accompaniment of much pistol cracking by the chum chosen to be best man at the wedding. And no wonder. If something wasn't needed to drown a Piedmontese maiden's cries at such a moment, she would be a stoic of the stoics.

Not the pistol but the sword gave fame to one

pair of earrings with royal associations. And all on account of a woman's doubt. Presented with a pair of pearl earrings by her husband, a certain Countess of Rheday would not believe the gems were real, so in exasperation the Count slashed at one of the pearls with his sword. "The mark of the cut is still visible" stated our present Queen's brother the Marquis of Cambridge in his will, when making "The Rheday Earrings" and the ornament they are now attached to as a pendant, an heirloom in the family of his eldest son.

THE EARRING

This is one of the oldest forms of personal ornament, and in the East was in use five thousand years ago. Recent excavations at Ur of the Chaldees yielded a gold earring from a man's tomb dated 2750 B.C. Much more ornate was a set of gold earrings from which tassels hung, found by Sir Flinders Petrie on the site of the Biblical city of Beth Paleth in Judea. Earrings of amber or rosin —it is not sure which—were found in Tut-ankh-Amen's tomb.

There is a legend which attributes the origin of earrings to Abraham, not for his own use but to deflect the jealousy of his wife Sarah from their bondmaid Hagar. Sarah declared that she would not rest until her hands had been imbued with Hagar's blood. Whereupon Abraham pierced

Hagar's ear quickly and drew a ring through it, so that Sarah was able to dip her hands in the blood of the bondmaid without bringing the latter into danger.

Earrings are the most frequently mentioned ornaments of Biblical times. Job's friends, when once his luck had turned, brought him "every man an earring of gold." When gold was being collected to make the Golden Calf the people were implored to "Break off the golden earrings which are in the ears of your wives, and of your sons and and of your daughters."

In very ancient Rome only women and slaves wore earrings. Then Julius Caesar set the fashion for freemen, and all the young bloods copied him.

Seven centuries ago the Sassanian kings of Persia were fond of wearing earrings, and thus adorned had their likenesses engraved on the precious stones which gemmed their signet rings.

Earrings have been found in the barrows or graves of our Anglo-Saxon forbears, so it is reasonable to suppose that such gewgaws were known in ancient Britain. There are medieval MSS to prove that earrings were worn in the Middle Ages, though the fashion in which women then did their hair, that is in long plaits falling down each side of the face, and the later fashion of covering the entire head, ears included, with a veil, or wimple, prevented any earrings being seen if they were worn.

The Elizabethan period saw the earring fashion well established in this island, and for men as well as women. 'Gloriana's' favourite, the Earl of Essex, wore earrings at Court. So did Shakespeare at the Globe Theatre.

The fashion continued on into the reign of the Stuarts. The first King Charles went to the scaffold wearing a pearl earring, a jewel which is now a treasure in the family of the Duke of Portland.

Chapter XI
FANTASTIC JEWELS

OF ALL the gifts showered upon Miss Amy Johnson to commemorate her lone flight to Australia, that from her native city of Hull—the silver globe of the world on which the continents are raised in gold—was the most rare.

Usually such 'baubles' are reserved for travellers of Royal rank; and probably the Duchess of York is Miss Johnson's only contemporary who possesses a more precious specimen of cartography. Her Royal Highness's silver map is of the Island of Mauritius, where she and the Duke went ashore on their trip to the Antipodes a few years ago. Diamonds mark the sugar factories on the island, a large sapphire the capital Port Louis, and rubies the string of lighthouses round the coast.

That maps can rank as fantastic jewels comes as no surprise after seeing the one in the Louvre which the Tzar of Russia thought a fitting gift to France at the time of the Franco-Russian Alliance. For that map is a mass of blazing gems on a groundwork of polished jasper, the jewels arranged to mark the various French provinces the names of which are inscribed in gold, while the principal rivers are indicated by strips of platinum.

Said to have cost in Russian roubles the equivalent of a quarter of a million English pounds, that map of France is only exceeded in value by a globe

of the world constructed to the order of a by-gone
Shah of Persia, and now catalogued among the
treasures in the Imperial Palace at Teheran. Sup-
ported by a column of diamonds, this specimen of
jewelled cartography with its seas represented by
emeralds and the continents by rubies, sapphires
and diamonds, has probably enlivened many a
Persian prince's path to learning.

That is before the advent of the present Shah.
He was peasant-born, and had been a trooper in a
Cossack regiment only twelve years before Fate
gave him the chance to seize the throne from an
effete and absentee ruler. But Riza Khan brought
a bevy of young sons to the royal palace who rank
as princes now, and they, maybe, have found the
jewelled globe a stimulus to imagination if not a
very adequate guide to world geography. For,
like the fantastically garbed statues that act as
lamp-posts round the ornamental lake in the palace grounds at Teheran, the jewelled globe is a
piece of eighteenth century craftsmanship, and
there has been much shuffling of national bounda-
ries since then, at all events, in Europe.

Jewels strange and rare were ever the delight of
kings and queens and princes, especially in the
Middle Ages in Europe. Perhaps it was that fantasy expressed in gold and gems helped to counter-
act the gloom of medieval castle and keep. Certainly Mary Queen of Scots both at Holyrood and
Fotheringay and also at Manor Castle, Sheffield,

got much cheer out of a curious jewel which her first husband the Dauphin of France gave her as a wedding present—a begemmed enamel figure of a boy trying to catch a mouse. That, and a little gold bird enamelled in green, together with a gold tortoise ruby encrusted, the gift of David Rizzio, were cherished by this unhappy royal lady to the end of her tragic life. She loved, too, to wear a pendant-jewel in the form of a tiny gold and enamelled Court fool with his cap and bells and bauble gemmed with diamonds and garnets and pearls, and inscribed on the back in Latin with the motto signifying, "He looks simple but he is not."

During her forty-five years reign Elizabeth of England acquired many treasures bright and beautiful, gifts of such being the best way of currying favour with a royal lady who had a constitutional craving for presents and liked them to be rich and rare. Four watches at least, the Earl of Leicester gave her, each more amazing in design than the last and more splendidly jewelled, —one was in a case of coloured enamel the shade and shape of a green apple.

After Elizabeth's death, many of her gewgaws were stowed away in what overseas visitors to London are apt to speak of as "the royal repository for jewelled junk," otherwise the Tower of London. Less than fifty years later, however, the Cromwellian Government decided to get rid of some of the nation's jewelled junk, and so, by Order of the

Council of State, an inventory was made and a-
mong the pieces selected for sale was a chessboard
inlaid with gold, silver, and pearls on which
'Gloriana' was said to have often pitted her skill
against that of her courtiers. Perhaps under a
Commonwealth the sentimental value of Royal
relics could hardly be expected to soar very high;
at all events £23 was all the royal lady's chessboard fetched. And at the same sale only £30 was
given for a "silver fountain for perfumed waters
artificially made to play by itself."

Once upon a time, and that not so very long ago,
figures of birds made in precious metals and precious stones had quite a vogue as gifts among royalty. Royal brides were given them and so were
royal bridesmaids. History tells that a silver peacock, the train of the bird set with pearls, sapphires
and rubies, was presented to Eleanor of Provence
when she married Henry II of France; biography
relates that a turquoise eagle with ruby eyes and
two pearls in its claws was given by Prince Albert
to Lady Ida Hay when acting as bridesmaid to
Queen Victoria.

And a royal diarist, Nicholas II the last of the
Russian Tzars, himself recorded of his marriage
to Princess Alice of Hesse —"While she was being
robed in the Malachite Drawing-room we waited
for her in the Arab Room . . . At ten minutes
past twelve (noon) the procession started for the
church, whence I returned a married man . . When

we were back in the Malachite Drawing-room the family presented us with an immense silver swan."

Most Russian monarchs had a flair for silverware, as the Silver Room in the Hermitage at Leningrad eloquently tells; Nicholas II developed a passion for goldware also. One of his most cherished possessions was a miniature model of the Imperial train which ran on the Trans-Siberian railway, the coaches complete with bathrooms, restaurant and private chapel, a gift from an admirer who knew well the Imperial penchant for goldsmithy. The last of the Tzars also liked to be given Easter eggs of gold, a liking his wife and family duly fostered. In that respect he rather resembled some of his predecessors' consorts, especially the eighteenth century Empress Elizabeth, one of whose surviving trinkets is a gold egg fitted with a watch, tweezers and tiny boxes, all bearing the royal owner's monogram in enamels.

Napoleon's generosity to Josephine in the matter of jewels is much stressed by his biographers, but his fondness for possessing precious bijouterie of his own is seldom mentioned. Yet he was intensely fastidious about his snuff-boxes and very partial to a pearl one. Nor without cause, seeing that to its fashioning went what is said to be the biggest baroque pearl in the world, while another, but little smaller pearl, formed the body of a frog, diamond-clawed and diamond-headed, crouched

on the lid as if surveying a meadow of green enamel grass starred with jewelled flowers. That unique
snuff-box is still in existence, the clou of a private
collection belonging to Captain William Ogden.
Even Catherine the Great never took snuff out of
a more rare container, though a snuff-box of hers
which fetched £2,600 at Christie's a few years ago
was ornate to a degree, with its floral sprays of diamonds superimposed on green jasper.

Baroque pearls have dominated other famous
trinkets besides Napoleon's snuff-box. Notably
the 'Canning Jewel' a sixteenth century pendant
ascribed to Benvenuto Cellini and once owned by
the King's son-in-law the Earl of Harewood, but
now a prized national possession thanks to the generosity of an anonymous American friend who
paid £10,000 for it when it was auctioned at
Sotheby's. The entire torso of the sea-god Triton,
which is the figure the pendant represents, is formed of a single baroque pearl, and its wonderful
sheen almost eclipses the rubies and diamonds and
the glint of translucent enamels in the sea-god's
tail. A rare jewel that, but not more so than another
credited with a Medici period in its history,—the
pendant of ambergris mounted in gold and jewelled, which is now in the Pierpont Morgan collection in New York. Design alone—a group of
children frolicking with their mother—would make
that pendant rare in an age when classical subjects
were the rage in all the arts, the goldsmith's no less

than the painter's; composed as it is of such a mysterious substance as the secretion of the sperm whale, the pendant is strange beyond compare.

Italian Renaissance jewels are much sought after by English collectors nowadays, partly because here in England the Renaissance influence manifested itself mainly in literature, whilst abroad its effects were felt in all the arts. Not without vision did Cosimo de Medici build shops on the Ponte Vecchio above the golden waters of the Arno specially for the Florentine artificers who wrought wondrously in precious metals. That alluring bridge of shops soon became the Mecca for artist-craftsmen anything but Italian-born, and they served Florence well not only by imbibing her new ideals of beauty but by broadcasting her other glories among the peoples of the lands whence they came.

Still, the Renaissance spirit, as it flared up in Italy, was not all-pervading all at once. The German goldsmiths, for instance, were slow to discard the religious symbolism which had for long characterised their work, and as late as near the end of the sixteenth century were making necklaces and other personal ornaments decorated with representations of Biblical subjects. One such necklace is in the Louvre, a string of wrought gold medallions jewelled with pearls and rubies, and exquisitely enamelled with scenes from the Passion. It is a superb specimen of sixteenth century German craftsmanship, and only in the style of its gold-smithy does it reveal traces of Italian influences.

Early seventeenth century jewellery was dominated by what has been termed the fauna and flora element in design, a vogue largely due to that wife whom James the Sixth of Scotland fetched out of Denmark and later brought to London to queen it in Whitehall when he came south to reign as James I of England. The accounts of George Herriot the Court Jeweller of that period, bristle with such items as "making a great ring in the form of a frog all sett with diamonds—£200," "making a pair of lizard pendants sett with diamonds," "making a daisy pendant," "making a bayleaf jewel with an opening for a picture," "making a Horn of Abundance sett with six rose diamonds and twelve table diamonds"—and many other fantastic personal ornaments all at the command of King James's Danish-born consort.

The seventeenth century was remarkable also in England for the beginnings of a vogue for memorial jewelry, some of which was fantastic to a gruesome degree. When Charles the First was beheaded, those of his devoted admirers who did not already possess some token of their attachment quickly set about getting one, and usually it was either a locket or a ring containing the ill-fated monarch's portrait backed by a skull and crossbones. One such Stuart memorial ring that the famous eighteenth century dilettante Horace

118

Walpole set great store by, bore between the initials C.R. on the front, the motto—"Prepared be to follow me." Whole skeletons were depicted on some memorial rings of this period, and were combined with such mottoes as "Remember Death," "Live to Die," "Breathe paine, death gaine." It was the French, however, who touched the heights —or depths—of the macabre in memorial jewellery when they produced a finger ring with a bezel shaped like a coffin, the lid of which could be raised by pressing a spring, so as to disclose a minute figure of Napoleon done in enamel.

But misunderstood monarchs and the "dear departed" have not been the sole inspiration of memorial jewels. When Sarah Bernhardt, the great French actress, was at the height of her fame she wore a trinket the like of which had not been seen before. It was a diamond in the shape of a tear, and had been presented to her by Victor Hugo after playing in *Rome Vaincue*. This jewel hung from a gold bracelet, and unfortunately the 'divine Sarah' lost it at a party given in her honour in London. Her host was very eager to replace the gem, but she declined the offer, saying "there could be no substitute for Victor Hugo's tear."

As might be expected of a country where its rulers have long been in the habit of spending fabulous sums on precious stones for their own or their favourites' bedizenment, India is not much behind Russia in its fame for fantastic jewels. And the State of Baroda harbours one of the most famous—a carpet of pearls with a diamond centre and diamond corners, which was intended by a bygone Maharajah for a Moslem lady to hang at the entrance to her purdah apartments. Alas! love may laugh at locksmiths but it rarely circumvents the priesthood, hence the tradition which attributes to religious differences the reason why that jewelled carpet has never left Baroda. Now, probably, it never will.

To come back to present-day England. Maps compounded of precious metals and precious stones are not for everybody, nor are they truly fantastic though rare enough to rank as strange with most people. But really fantastic jewels are being created nowadays, as certain post-war exhibitions in London have revealed. When that jewel-artist Mr Lyndhurst Pocock showed his work at a Bond street Gallery, the Press and public alike went into raptures over a pear-shaped pendant of amber carved into the exquisite semblance of a water-babe astride upon a dolphin.

Chapter XII
ROYAL KEEPSAKES

AMONG the cherished personal possessions of the exiled Queen of Spain there is, or used to be when she dwelt in a palace in Madrid, a small china box shaped like a fan. It came to her Majesty from her godmother the ex-Empress Eugenie of France, and had seemed a strangely insignificant token to be named in the Empress's Last Will and Testament as the sole bequest to one who was regarded as her favourite grandchild. Yet what a wonderful keepsake the china box turned out to be. When unlocked it revealed a tiara of emeralds and diamonds!

Why the jewels had not been bequeathed openly in the ordinary way, is explained by a biographer as due to the Empress's love of practical joking. Even unto very old age—this royal lady lived to be ninety-four—her zest for playing pranks remained unimpaired, sometimes with results extremely disconcerting to members of her household.

Still, nobody expected this idiosyncrasy to characterise the Empress's will, her god-daughter least of all. But if Queen Ena of Spain had felt any chagrin at being named in a legal document for the apparently paltry gift of a china box, such chagrin must have changed to pleasurable surprise when she found what the box concealed.

Emeralds and diamonds! Always these had

been the Empress Eugenie's favourite gems. And little wonder. For not only did they suit her better than any other jewels but they were the first keepsake she received from Napoleon III. And that before he had offered her marriage! Discreetly chaperoned the beauteous blonde Spaniard had been walking with the swarthy French Emperor in the forest of Compiègne when she had stopped to admire a clover leaf glittering with dew. Next day that masterpiece of Nature's handiwork came to her reproduced in jewels—a clover leaf of emeralds bespattered with dewdrops of diamonds. At the command of the Emperor his confidential friend Count Bacchiochi had journeyed to Paris to search for such a trinket.

Not all royal keepsakes of interest to historians have been bestowed in such felicitous circumstances. Queen Marie Antoinette was practically a prisoner in the Tuileries when she sent to the Princesse de Lamballe a ring containing a lock of her hair with the inscription—"Bleached by Sorrow." Few queens ever had a more devoted woman-friend than had the wife of Louis XVI of France in this Princess, and that ring brought her to the Queen's side in double quick time. But what a piteous reminder of the carefree years when the royal lady's hair had been bleached by a less painful process.

Time is not always kind to keepsakes, but there did survive the frenzy of the French Revolution

A ROYAL KEEPSAKE : THE IVORY PIQUE NECKLACE PRESENTED BY
QUEEN MARIE ANTOINETTE TO THE PRINCESS DE LAMBALLE.

By permission of the Trustees of the Wallace Collection.

To face page 122.]

in another relic of the wonderful friendship between these two tragic-fated women—a necklace of ivory beads wrought with fleur-de-lys in gold pique work. A gift from the Queen to the Princess in the days when they were young and light-hearted together, that necklace now serves to remind posterity of what loyalty brought upon a woman. Personally, I can never look at it in the Wallace Collection, London, without seeing with my mind's eye a maniacal mob striking down Madame Lamballe on the very threshold of the prison La Force, stripping her naked and ripping the heart out of her body to carry it on a pike—her head hoisted upon another—through the blood-streaming streets of Paris.

One sometimes wonders whether France resents England's possession of that relic so closely entwined with French history. Perhaps not, the relic being royal. And there is this to be said in justification of its being here instead of there—the necklace was acquired in open purchase by an English nobleman, the fourth Marquis of Hertford, while he was domiciled in Paris and making greater benefactions to the land of his adoption than to the land of his birth. All the same the ivory workers in present-day Dieppe claim that such an historic specimen of their craft ought to be treasured in Paris, at the Louvre or the Cluny.

Far from the country of its origin went another keepsake bestowed by Marie Antoinette—the massive gold ring set with a catseye, which that royal lady gave to her devoted admirer Count Axel de Fersen when they parted on the road to Varennes. It was not the first ring the French queen had given the young Swede—there had been that other gold circlet engraved with three fleur-de-lys and the words "Honi à ceux qui les abandonne" which she had sent him by the Prince Esterhazy and had herself worn two days to make it the more dear and personal to the recipient. The catseye ring had an even greater significance, being a token of hope in future meetings. Alas! Count Fersen only saw Marie Antoinette once again and then he was powerless to aid her. Having planned the flight of the Royal Family to Varennes and seen them well on their way, Fersen left them, as agreed, at a certain stage of the journey. Thenceforward the going did not keep according to schedule, there were delays, with the result that the royal fugitives were overtaken and had to turn back. The rest, with the guillotine at the end, is common knowledge. Eventually Count Fersen returned to the land of his birth where he rose to high favour at the Court of Gustavus the Fourth. Always he wore Marie Antoinette's parting gift; it gleamed on his left hand when he was stoned to death on the steps of Stockholm cathedral while attending the funeral of the young Swedish prince whom rumour said he had poisoned to make way for another dynasty.

Nor does the legend of that royal keepsake end there. The sight of the catseye ring on the dead Count's finger so infuriated a fisherman in the mob that he hacked it off—finger and all—with an axe and flung it far out to sea. But, if legend is to be believed, Nemesis awaited him. For, next evening, while fishing, he saw the ring gleaming on a distant rock and, compelled by some mysterious force, he picked it up. Then to his horror, he saw a hand, a hand intact, grasping the mast above his head. Presently the hand relaxed its hold and disappeared into the Baltic. When the fisherman returned to Stockholm he was mad.

One of the most poignantly interesting royal love tokens known is the mourning ring of the third Mary Stuart. Whoever dreamt, when the phlegmatic William Prince of Orange married the simple sixteen-years-old daughter of James II of England, that eventually a strand of the bride's hair, imprisoned beneath a chip of crystal, would be the greatest solace of the bridegroom during the last eight years of his life? Certainly not Prince William, for he made no effort to win the affection of the girl whom he had married. But Fate had a say in the matter, and ultimately gave that royal pair more marital felicity than usually befell such exalted folk thenadays.

The little jewel which tells the tale of the royal widower's grief and proves how richly brown the royal lady's tresses were, is now in Canada, an heirloom possession of the Wallace family of West-borough, Ontario. The present owner's description of it written for Miss Marjorie Bowen's biographical study "The Third Mary Stuart," shows the ring to have been quite in the fashion of the memorial jewellery of the period with its skull and cross-bones. "The jewel," writes Mr J. N. Wallace, "is very peculiar, being a slightly oval setting of a ring, seven-eighths of an inch wide, the marks where the hoop was attached being quite visible. The groundwork is hair, closely plaited, in the centre a monogram G.M.R. surmounted by a crown, with an orb on each side, and below a skull and cross-bones, all beautifully worked in fine gold wire. Around the outer zone are the words "Memento Maria regina obit 28 December 1694." The whole is covered with glass or crystal fitted like a watch-glass. It seems the King first wore it as a locket, as there is a small eyelet attached at one edge, so placed that, when worn round the neck on a long ribbon and lifted by the hand, the jewel is viewed right side up."

An earlier and more ill-fated Stuart, that Charles who ended his days on a scaffold in White-hall and is now known as the Martyr King, seems to have been responsible for the vogue of wearing hair jewellery in token of remembrance. At all events prior to his execution King Charles I gave a lock of his hair enclosed in a silver heart, to each of "twelve loyal gentlemen" and one of those twelve lockets is still in existence, treasured, so I am assured, by the Wetherall family of Pang-bourne-on-Thames.

A hundred years later another royal Stuart, 'Bonnie Prince Charlie, the Young Pretender,' also rewarded loyalty with a locket. But this time it was a golden locket and it contained not a lock of the donor's hair but his portrait. It was all Charles had to offer Flora Macdonald for conveying him, disguised as an Irish spinning maid, from Benbecula in the Outer Hebrides to the Isle of Skye and there sheltering him overnight. But she thought more of that locket than the £1,500 presented to her after her subsequent imprisonment in the Tower of London. The little royal keepsake went with her across the Atlantic when she emigrated with her husband to North Carolina. Nor did the years there dim her memories of that parting with the Prince at Portree, or blunt her sympathies with the Stuart cause. She was still an ardent Jacobite when circumstances brought her back to the homeland; and when death came to her she was buried in the sheet Prince Charlie had slept in that fateful night on Skye.

Peculiarly pathetic are the circumstances associated with another celebrated royal keepsake—the ring which George III of England was given by his youngest—and thirteenth—child, the Princess Amelia. Perhaps because she was the thirteenth comer to the royal nursery she was never very strong, and the streak of melancholy in her disposition was probably fostered by the knowledge of her brother the Prince of Wales's dissipated way of life, and her father's mental lapses. Yet there never was any lack of affection between her and the King, and it was for him, and not her mother Queen Charlotte, that this Princess in her last illness, had a ring made to contain a tress of her hair set under a crystal rimmed with tiny diamonds.

To that Princess's brother the notorious Prince of Wales belongs the fame of having inspired what is perhaps the most curious royal keepsake in history— the miniature of a woman's eye, Mrs Fitzherbert's eye, set in a gold locket. Whosoever idea it was, the royal lover's or his inamorata's, it was a quaint and touching conceit, and the expression of it in paint on ivory by Richard Cosway heightened the renown of that already renowned miniaturist. A lovely eye it certainly was, large, lambent and soft, just as one would have expected in a woman of Mrs Fitzherbert's character and disposition. That such a keepsake should be treasured for more than forty years and be worn in death by the man who repudiated his marriage with its giver and had many mistresses before he expired a wornout debauchee at sixty-eight, only goes to show how labyrinthine are the secret places of the human heart.

Nobody could accuse Queen Victoria or the Prince Consort of letting their affections stray from each other, but this Queen certainly once sent a keepsake to a man who was not her husband. True, the recipient was old enough to be her father, but that detail would not have saved any queen's reputation at other Courts in other days. Even now the letter which accompanied the gift could easily be misconstrued by a foreigner who knew nothing of Queen Victoria's private life and public career. "The Queen sends the little charm," wrote her Majesty from Windsor Castle in October 1839, "which she hopes will keep Lord Melbourne from *all evil*, and which it will make her very happy if he will put it with his keys. If the ring is too small Lord Melbourne must send it back to her and she will have it altered."

Lord Melbourne's acknowledgment of that royal token is not on record. But his joy in it can be surmised from a note in the Greville Diaries. "I have no doubt," wrote Greville, "that he (Lord Melbourne) is passionately fond of her (Queen Victoria) as he might be of his daughter if he had one, and the more because he is a man with a capacity for loving without having anything in the world to love."

Some royal keepsakes there are with a special interest for students of social history because they are keepsakes twice over. One such is the ruby brooch and pendant which our present Queen Mary wears in memory of the late Countess Torby who married the Grand Duke Michael of Russia;

129

another is a small gilt and jewelled cabinet bearing the inscription "Charles I to Henrietta Maria," which Constance Lady Battersea left to Queen Mary with her "respectful and loyal duty." And as all the world knows from her own telling, Frances Countess of Warwick received as a keepsake from King Edward when he was Prince of Wales, the gold ring inscribed "Gott mit Dir" which Queen Victoria and the Prince Consort gave to their eldest son on the occasion of his confirmation.

Sentiment is supposed to be the very essence of all keepsakes royal or otherwise, but inordinate ambition is known to have inspired the princely presentation of one. When the Duke of Brabant who made history as Leopold II of the Belgians returned from one of his voyages to the East, he brought back as a souvenir to Frere-Orban, then Minister of Finance, a stone picked up among the majestic ruins of the Acropolis at Athens, and upon this fragment he had had engraved the words —"Belgium must have a colony."

Chapter XIII
TREASURES OF JADE

JADE is ranked by the Chinese as the most precious of precious stones. To them it is what diamonds are to western peoples, and it has enjoyed Imperial favour since long before the Christian era. When China first began to be represented at the Courts of Europe, her Ambassadors' womenfolk always wore jade ornaments on great occasions, and even now the wife of the Chinese Minister accredited to Great Britain never attends a Royal Court at Buckingham Palace without a double string of jade beads rippling down the front of the brocade coat which is part of her national costume.

But—and there is a but with regard to the estimation in which jade is held by the Chinese—it is nearly always worn in conjunction with pearls. A pair of priceless emerald-green jade earrings—rings within hanging from three large beautiful pearls—were among the few personal jewels which the wife of the young ex-Emperor of China was able to take out of the Forbidden City in Peking when she and her husband were banished in 1923. The famous Empress-Dowager Tzu-Hsi also habitually wore earrings of jade combined with pearls; hers, however, were stud earrings and the pearls rimmed the jade. She was, too, passionately fond of jade bracelets, often wearing two on each wrist and invariably she slept in a pair. She wore jade rings also, and finger-nail protectors of jade, the latter three inches long. All these as a matter of course. For great occasions such as a garden party at the Summer Palace for the foreign diplomats in Peking, she would don a shoulder cape of pearls fringed with jade pendants and fastened with clasps of jade.

For three thousand years jade has been one of the most cherished substances carried by the camel caravans that traverse the ancient jade routes across the roof of the world by way of the Jade Gate, a narrow opening in that strangest of all testimonies to human fear, the Great Wall of China. Quarried in Khotan in Chinese Turkestan, jade has to travel fifteen hundred miles before it reaches the famous lapidaries of Peking.

Jade, the scientist tells us, is a mixture of silicate of chalk and magnesium; according to the poets it is the crystallisation of the sea-emerald's spirit. Whatever the Chinese lapidary thinks of jade he has to bring an infinity of patience and generations of inherited skill to the manipulation of it. For jade is a quartz nearly as hard as a diamond, and its cutting and engraving are not to be undertaken lightly or wantonly. Some of the greygreen jade boxes of the K'ien Lung period so sought after by rich European connoisseurs, took years to carve. They are things of lyrical beauty with their linings of gold lacquer, and their pierced lids through which came the perfume of the sweet scented spices they were designed to contain.

Jade varies enormously in colour. Centuries ago the Chinese tabulated nine different kinds including a wonderful kingfisher-blue now so rare as to be met with only in museums. Of fine white jade were the two tiny figurines which accompanied the pair of emerald-green jade necklaces sent by the Republican Government of China to the King of England's daughter on her marriage in 1922. That same white jade was much favoured by the mandarins of old for their elaborately carved jade wine ewers.

Ah! those mandarins! What sybarites they were, what connoisseurs in the art of living. They would give a thousand ounces of silver for a pair of bracelets of emerald-green jade, twice as much for a pair of jade chopsticks mounted in gold. They, even more than their womenfolk, appraised jade for something no westerner seeks for in diamonds —the exquisite pleasure to be got out of fingering it. Much as they loved to feast their eyes on jade they loved better to caress it, and would carry a piece about with them in their sleeves to "feel" in moments of leisure. Moreover they trained their finger-tips to that special purpose. So did their Manchu rulers. It is told of the Empress-Dowager Tzu-Hsi that early in life she started the daily habit of rolling little round pebbles over and over in a lacquer bowl of tepid scented water in order to become proficient in the subtle art of 'feeling jade.' Nor did she drop the habit when the cares and responsibilities of statecraft pressed heavily upon her. Indeed it grew to be her favourite relaxation as she rested on the lovely marble terrace above the lotus-fringed lake at her Summer Palace thirteen miles out of Peking. Thus did she keep up her reputation for being the best judge of jades in China, able to tell one colour from another in the dark, to know at a touch whether a jade was grey-green, sea-green or emerald-green, brown, red-black, or kingfisher-blue or her own favourite mutton-fat white.

Those were the great days of jade. It did not then, as now under a Republic, depend on woman for its prestige in the realm of personal ornament. Men wore it. True, they usually did so in prescribed forms which indicated their rank or official standing, but a string of jade beads worn as a badge by a man can be no less ornamental than one worn by a woman at the dictates of her own will and fancy. In Imperial China the feather in the cap of a high military personage would be held in place by a piece of jade that might have cost as much as two thousand pounds though not measuring more than two inches high, while the correct girdle-clasp for a Manchu Court dignitary would be of jade rimmed with rubies. As for the girdle of the Emperor himself, it was ornamented with plaques of jade which varied with the occasion—

yellow for rites at the Altar of Earth, white jade
for the Altar of the Moon. Up to the beginning of
the Manchu dynasty there were as many as twenty
four jade plaques on the Emperor's girdle. And
when his Majesty journeyed from one palace to
another he rode in a lacquer chariot decorated
with panels of jade.

To Chinese people jade symbolises Eternity
and Longevity; and all the important vessels of
the ancient temple and the chief treasures of the
Imperial Court have been fashioned of fine jade
One empress of the Han dynasty wore a crown of
jade; and a dazzling diadem it must have been,
fashioned as it was out of bright green jade with
upright lobes carved in the form of cloud scrolls
inlaid with pieces of yellow, red, green and white
jade encrusted with pearls. More than a thousand
years ago another empress used a jade hook to
gather mulberry leaves with when rearing silk-
worms, a hook as fine as a bent sinew and mounted
on a gold handle.

And ever since the art of carving jade has been
practised in China, the ceremonial wine-cups used
in the nuptial rites of members of the Imperial
House, have been of jade. One of the loveliest objects in the Bishop Collection of Jade at the Metropolitan Museum of Art, New York, is a marriage
wine-cup of carved white jade tinged with palest
green, that is believed to have served nearly all the
Imperial brides and bridegrooms of the Manchu

dynasty, as well it may have done considering the quality of the jade, its exquisite workmanship and the fact that the cup came into foreign hands after the looting of the Summer Palace in 1860.

Confucius saw in jade the symbols of intelligence, justice, humanity and harmony, and Chinese people attribute these qualities to their friends when they send them tiny jade sceptres in token of good will. Ju'i or 'As you like it' sceptres they are called, and they used to be permissible presents from one royalty to another, and even between royalty and persons of less exalted station. So it was quite in keeping with Chinese good manners for the Emperor Kuang-hsu to send Queen Victoria of England a jade sceptre mounted in rubies, on the occasion of her Jubilee, and not surprising that among the bequests named in the will of a onetime British Ambassador to Peking should be a "jade sceptre in ornamental case presented to me by the Dowager Empress of China."

In earlier times these jade sceptres, modelled in the natural form of a branching stem of the sacred fungus *ling-chih* were often among the presents made to China's emperors by officials who served the Throne in the various provinces—or were supposed to serve it. Sometimes, however, loyalty lagged far behind the sceptred jade. Once, when that happened during the nineteenth century, the then Emperor Chia Ch'ing did a little plain speaking. "It has been your custom," said the Imperial decree, "to present me with jade sceptres of good luck which I have invariably returned to the donors. The recent conspiracy certainly does not denote good luck, and I beg that my officials will offer me no more such 'luck' tokens."

Once upon a time, too, in China, jade was presented for 'luck' to the Imperial princesses on their marriage. But then it usually took the form of discs engraved with appropriate legends to hang on their bed-curtains. And when the babies came, which they should fast and often if the jade marriage-tokens had been true to tradition, other jade offerings would be made on the occasion of the babe's First Ceremonial Bath, that important event when, at a month old he is introduced to the world at large and given his first Milk Name.

One emperor under the T'ang dynasty used always, whenever an Imperial child was born in the palace, to send jade money with the customary sliced fruit as baby-washing gifts of good augury, the "money" being inscribed with prayers for prosperity. And it is told of another emperor that when a great-grandson was born to him he presented the infant with a set of jade mountains carved with hares and tassels. Thus were Imperial children early taught to appreciate in jade both beauty of substance and delicacy of craftsmanship.

As in birth, so in death, jade was essential to ancient Chinese symbolism. In far off days and long ago Imperial princes and anyone rich enough to afford it, were buried with eyes, mouth, nostrils, ears—all the apertures of the body—closed up by means of jade as a protection to the deceased against the ravages of the elements. Tomb amulets, such jades were called, and their manufacture was a special craft among the lapidaries of Peking during the Han dynasty. Nowadays such jades are the quest of the archeologists, though less learned folk will prize one as a lucky thing to have about the house.

Jade, too, had its significance in the ritual of religious and social observances. Circular-shaped discs of jade were used in the worship of the deity of the heavens, square-shaped discs in the worship of the diety of earth. A jade disc could also be a token of re-union and as such was often sent from friend to friend instead of a letter. *Au contraire* a jade disc with a segment cut out, was a delicate intimation of a forthcoming separation.

Perhaps because the ancient annals told of emperors who, when preparing for great sacrificial rites were fed only on jade dissolved in aromatic wine, some Chinese encyclopaedias of more recent date announce that jade, when powdered to the size of rice grains, would strengthen the heart, lungs and vocal organs. Whether or no such a belief is held in the twentieth century, jade is still credited with power to influence health, so that during the hot summer months well-to-do people in Peking carry about with them discs of brown-

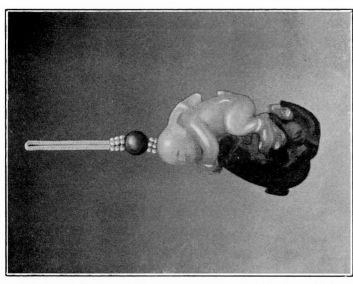

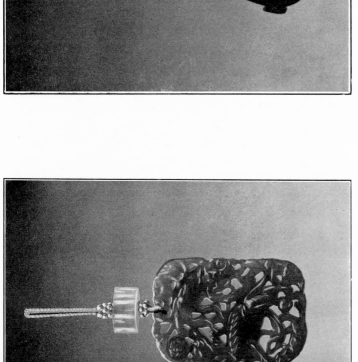

CHINESE JADE AMULETS.

Amulet carved to represent a lion, a lioness and   Figure of a boy sculptured in white jade standing
young lions. The lion or tiger denoted, in China,   on a sea-dragon in black jade.
mandarin rank.

By courtesy of Messrs. Liberty & Co., Ltd., Regent Street.

To face page 138.]

flecked jade to ward off disease. Lady Hosie, in her delightful *Portrait of a Chinese Lady* tells of her father being presented with such a 'magic' piece of jade by a high-born Chinese maiden, who slipped it into the elderly Englishman's waistcoat pocket with a maternal smile and a gentle word of admonition that he must not lose it.

Some of the most fascinating of ancient jade amulets are in the form of pendants carved with Chinese characters signifying 'good fortune.' One such adorned the watch-chain of ex-King George of Greece before he presented it to the little Princess Elizabeth of York who now wears it dangling from a bracelet. Dragons used to be—and still are —a favourite form of decoration on amulets of jade, for in China a dragon is not regarded as the fearsome beast which English people think it, but as a benevolent creature capable of exercising useful and beneficent powers. Especially is it the symbol of fertilising rain, which means much to an agricultural people like the Chinese. But the peony and the pomegranate run the dragon close for popularity, the one symbolising happiness and the other an abundance of offspring, and the two together deemed the ideal decoration for a jade amulet intended for a woman's wear.

Treasures of Jade! Here in the West some of the finest that are not in museums are in Buckingham Palace. Tallies several of them are, credentials sent with Imperial missives from the Court of China to

Queen Victoria of England. Not that they were then appreciated at the Court of St. James for what they were, either intrinsically or symbolically, else they would never have been stowed away in cupboards at Windsor Castle and forgotten until King Edward came to the throne and had them routed out.

Even he, however, was not a connoisseur and a collector, and therefore never added to his heritage of jade. That honour rests with his daughter-in-law, Queen Mary. And her Majesty, being knowledgeable about Chinese art, and her taste impeccable, has made additions which, say the experts, hold their own easily with the jades which were the gifts of by-gone emperors and empresses of China.

Chapter XIV
CROWNS OF HISTORY AND MYSTERY

PRECIOUS metals and precious stones do not compose every royal diadem. Iron and steel went to the making of Roumania's. Dull and unattractive? By no means! For what that crown lacks in glitter it makes up for in symbolism, it having been fashioned out of the molten remains of cannon captured at the battle of Plevna; and Plevna, as all the Near East knows, freed Roumania from Turkish dominion.

Still, pictorially, the king's crown certainly played second fiddle to the queen's at the coronation of King Ferdinand and Queen Marie of Roumania at Alba Julia in 1922. And little wonder. For hers was of gold, purest yellow Transylvanian gold beaten into classic arabesques and set with moonstones, amethysts, turquoises, emeralds and rubies, all highly polished but not facetted. Moreover it had dangling discs that hid her Majesty's pretty ears and terminated in trefoils that swept below her shoulders. Which was all as it should be, Queen Marie having had her crown copied from the crown of that Despina Doanna, the wife of the Prince of Wallachia whom you may see to-day pictured in the frescoes of the ancient church of Curtea d'Argesh two hours journey from Bucharest.

If Roumania had her way she would be able to show another crown besides the iron one as a symbol of her sovereignty. Alas! the pearl-studded and enamelled silver-gilt diadem she covets is in the Vienna National Museum and Austria does not seem inclined to part with it, not even for cash. Twice, since 1925, Roumania has offered to buy it. But Austria is between two conflicting claims. Roumania wants the crown because it was worn by Prince Stephen Bocskay of Transylvania who, three centuries ago, ruled territory much of which is now Roumanian, and Hungary objects because that very territory belonged to her.

So, in all probability the crown will remain in Vienna and continue to swell the marvellous collection of priceless treasures which was famous long before the days of the Dual Monarchy. Indeed if Austria let that historic relic go she might feel in duty bound to surrender another—the iron and copper helmet of Albania's national hero, Skanderbeg the Great. Already Albania has made one application for it—in 1928 when President Ahmed Zogu was about to be proclaimed king as Skanderbeg III.

A propos of crowns that have strayed far from the scenes of their early splendour, that of Abyssinia was possessed by Britain for fifty years, and has only recently been restored to the land where it rightly belongs. Originally made for the famous Emperor Theodore, it was taken as loot at the storming of Magdala, and sold by a British soldier to a Prussian officer who sent it as a gift to his own sovereign. After that for about twelve months it reposed in Berlin, and might have remained in Germany to this day had not negotiations between that country and ours ended in its coming to London and the South Kensington Museum. As crowns go Abyssinia's is not old, dating back less than two hundred and fifty years, though it is a copy of European work of the sixteenth century. More gold than jewels went to its making, but the gold, being pierced to a pattern was ornamental enough of itself. When this crown was restored to Abyssinia in 1925 a brand new throne went with it, also as a gift from England, both being conveyed from the coast to the interior by bullock cart closely guarded by a mounted Indian escort.

English crowns, too, have had their ups and downs. King John's was lost in the Lincoln Washes, with the result that his young son Henry III was crowned with the gold throat collar belonging to his mother, a ceremony that took place in Gloucester Cathedral when the lad was but nine. True, England possessed another royal crown, that of Edward the Confessor, but it was far distant in London, and Isabelle of Angoulême, John's widow, thought that the sooner John's son went through a coronation ceremony the better for his security, to say nothing of her own. Queen Philippa's crown also made history that sounds romantic at this distance of time, for it was in pawn at Cologne for three years, and had to be redeemed by the people of England subscribing thirty thousand packs of wool specially for the purpose! Indeed Philippa and her husband Edward III were constantly hard up because they nearly always had a war on, and during their reign the crown jewels were seldom out of pawn.

Three centuries later came the most exciting happening to the English crown. There was actually an attempt to steal it from the Tower of London. And the bandits got away with it, too—as far as the drawbridge. But were they punished for their treason? Not a bit of it! Charles the Second was king then, and he seems to have been more amused than alarmed by the crime. At all events he forgave Captain Blood, the ringleader, and even rewarded him with a gift of lands for his daring. Only the poor Keeper of the Tower seems to have suffered by the episode, all he got being a bashing about the head from the bandits when he cried out for help at seeing them rifling the glass case in which the crown was kept.

Charles did better by the Scots minister and his wife who saved the crown jewels of Scotland during the period when he was banished from Britain. For at the Restoration he got Parliament to grant them a sum of "two thousand merks Scots" for "conveying the royal honours, his Majesty's crown, sceptre and sword out of Dunnottar Castle

before it was rendered to the English Usurpers"
and taking care that the same "was hid and preserved." And right well they had earned the reward. Especially Mrs Grainger. For she had rid-
den through the English blockading army with
the crown concealed in her lap, "her maid following on foot with the sceptre and sword done up in
bundles of lint which Mrs Grainger pretended
were to be spun into thread." Still, the husband's
co-operation was necessary, as the Countess
Dowager Keith well knew when she devised the
scheme. So the Rev. James Grainger, minister of
Kineff, "raised the pavement stone just before the
pulpit, in the night tyme, and digged under it one
hole and put them (the crown and sceptre) in there,
and filled up the hole and layed down the stone
just as it was before . . . and, at the west end of the
church among some common seits digged down
in the ground and laid the case containing it (the
sword) and covered it up, so removing the super-
fluous mould it could not be discerned by anybody.

Odd mischances have befallen other royal
crowns. The very diadem which Roumania has
offered to buy from Austria was once lost on a
journey when the monarch took it with him to go
awooing in a distant country, with the result that
the royal would-be suitor was cast into prison because he had no crown available to prove his kingly status. Luckily it was found before his majesty
had been long in durance vile, whereupon the

father-in-law-to-be made the amende honorable and bestowed his daughter with his blessing.

Later, at the hands of the widowed queen of King Albert of Hungary, that particular crown suffered many indignities for safety's sake. On one occasion when the royal lady was beset by Polish insurgents she turned the crown upside down and stuck a spoon in it to make it look like her babe's saucepan. Then she popped it into the babe's cradle with the bedding banked around it. After that the crown was sewn into a red velvet cushion and one of the queen's ladies sat upon it during a sleigh ride across the frozen Danube.

Nor was that the end of this diadem's vicissitudes. In the middle of the nineteenth century the Hungarian dictator Louis Kossuth contrived to get possession of it, and thereafter for three years it was lost to the world. Eventually it was dug up in a field near Orsova. But not before Kossuth had laid plans for despatching it to England, plans which went agley through a friend's chance remark, a remark which gave the Austrian government a clue to the crown's whereabouts.

Spain possesses a crown that lay buried underground twelve hundred years. It is the diadem of Swinthila, King of the Visigoths who reigned in Spain during the seventh century. Fear of invasion by the Saracens is thought to have been the reason for its being hidden, along with ten other diadems, in a subterranean vault at La Fuente de

Guarrazar near Toledo. A great storm of torrential rain in 1858 was the known cause of the accidental discovery of this treasure, a peasant working in the fields was the lucky finder, and a present and a pension from Queen Isabella II his ultimate reward.

Not quite in accordance with present-day notions of what is befitting royalty, seems that ancient crown. For though pure gold fashions it, and the precious gems, sapphires and pearls, embellish it, what is merely red glass enters into its make-up. The red glass, however, appears in a part of the crown absent from more modern diadems, being inset into the open letters of gold which fringe the forehead band and spell the name of the king for whom the crown was made. Eight similar crowns that belonged to later Visigoth royalties, are in the Cluny Museum at Paris, having been purchased by the French Government for four thousand pounds. And all, like that of King Swinthila, which is treasured in the Real Armeria at Madrid, have evidently been votive offerings at some period to a church, as was the custom, for attached to the upper rim of each crown are chains whereby to suspend it.

One of the earliest crowns known to have been actually worn by a Spanish monarch was that made in the fifteenth century for the joint coronation of King Ferdinand and Queen Isabella, and was of gold with eight leaves prominent in the de-

sign and many precious stones by way of embellishment. That crown was not closed with arches
until the marriage of Phillip II of Spain with
Queen Mary of England, about a century later.
But how rarely it was worn! For, since the weld-
ing together of Spain's fourteen provinces into
one kingdom, there has been no actual coronation
ceremony in Spain, the accession of a new monarch being signified by his taking the royal oath
in the presence of his Ministers.

Yet that is not to say that crowns have never
graced State ceremonies. Spanish queens-consort
usually had crowns officially prepared for them—
that for Queen Mercedes, the first wife of Alfonso
XII was ornamented with five thousand brilliants.
And when a later King Alfonso announced his betrothal to the English Princess Ena of Battenberg,
the ladies of Catalonia suggested that they should
offer the royal bride a jewelled coronet. And a
rather remarkable coronet it proved to be, in that
its design embodied the Arms of England and the
fleurs-de-lys of the House of Bourbon, with the
four bars of Catalonia inset with rubies and diamonds.

What is probably the most revered crown in
Europe belongs to Italy and is known as the Iron
Crown of Lombardy. Not that its strikes the be-
holder as iron on first seeing it carried in procession
round the fifteenth century cathedral at Monza.
To all outward seeming the crown is of gold—six

gold plates hinged one to another with gold wire and studded with jewels above a rim of translucent emerald-green enamel. But within the circlet is a narrow strip of iron, made, so legend says, by hammering out a nail that had pierced Christ on the Cross. Thus does the crown get its name, and thus arose the tradition that has made the crown an object of veneration for hundreds of years.

In Monza they tell you that this crown was presented to a duke of Turin in the sixth century and that it was made by order of Theodolinda the widowed queen of Authoris King of Lombardy. Historians and antiquarians however doubt this, especially the antiquarians, who assert that the crown is of Byzantine workmanship, and that the art of enamelling had not penetrated to Italy in Queen Theodolinda's time.

Be that as it may, it is certainly one of the oldest crowns in the world and the smallest. For the circlet is only six inches wide, not wide enough to fit the head of a two-years-old child, let alone that of a grown man. So it is thought to have been a votive crown, and only used in coronations as a symbol, by being held above the head of a new monarch. Not that coronations have been its only great days of glory. A burial has added lustre to its name. For in 1878 the Iron Crown of Lombardy was the most striking feature in the grand cortege which followed the remains of King Victor Emmanuel to the Pantheon at Rome. And on its journey across Italy from Monza, escorted by the corporation and chapter of that cathedral city, it had everywhere been received with royal honours.

Another remarkable crown around which has gathered a good deal of history and mystery is that of the Holy Roman Empire, a diadem now in Vienna's keeping. If one of Albert Durer's pictures were anything to go by, that crown would be the crown of the Frankish Emperor Charlemagne for it appears in Durer's painting of that great monarch. As a matter of historic fact and antiquarian research Charlemagne's crown was never preserved, although French tradition claimed as Charlemagne's the diadem used in the coronations of the kings of France down to the time of Louis the Sixteenth. "The archbishop of Rheims took from the altar the crown of Charlemagne which had been brought from the Abbey of St. Denis, and placed it on the king's head" wrote Madame Campan in her *Memoirs of Marie Antoinette*. And she goes on to describe the crown as of "gold enriched with rubies and sapphires; it is lined with a crimson cap embroidered with gold and surmounted by a golden fleur-de-lys covered with six Oriental pearls."

Yet if that were really Charlemagne's crown why is the Louvre exhibit of Napoleon's crown, which was supposed to be a copy of Charlemagne's, ornamented with nothing but antique cameos and intaglios? At all events neither Louis the Six-

teenth's nor Napoleon's crown tallies with the one
depicted by Albert Durer in his imaginary portrait of Charlemagne. Actually this fifteenth century German artist immortalised in paint a diadem bearing the name of the eleventh century Holy
Roman Emperor Conrad II, which is the jewel in
Vienna.

And a peculiarly interesting crown it is. For
four of its eight panels are enamelled with figures
of Christ and the Biblical kings David, Solomon
and Hezekiah, clad in byzantine costumes and
each named on a testamentary scroll. Antiquarian
authority claims that this crown is made up of portions belonging to two different epochs. Be that as
it may it is a crown of rare design, and because of
its associations with the ancient Roman-German
Empire, was taken for the model of the crown
made for the first German Emperor in 1871. But
on the newer diadem there were no figures of
Christ, David, Solomon and Hezekiah; instead
appeared spread eagles with a star above.

Not all crowns are round. The ancient historical
crowns of Russia that used to be preserved in the
Kremlin at Moscow, were dome-shaped. And the
rich gold plates, barbarically jewelled, of which
they were composed, sprang from a broad brow-
band of sable fur, as if there were occasions, less
exalted than a coronation, when the crowns would
have to be worn out of doors during the rigors of a
Russian winter. The crown made for Catherine I

—hers was the first Imperial coronation—had no fur about it judging by the contemporary pictures in which it was depicted. Neither had the crown of Catherine II—Catherine the Great—the exquisite mitre-shaped diadem made by the celebrated French jeweller Jeremie Pozier from gems extracted from various Imperial ornaments declared not in accordance with eighteenth century taste. In Catherine the Great's crown, which is the one worn by all subsequent Muscovite monarchs and as recently as 1906 when Nicholas II opened the Duma with it on his head, there are five thousand diamonds and only one coloured stone, the ruby spinel beneath the diamond cross placed at the very top.

But perhaps Persia's crown is the strangest to western eyes. For it is shaped like a flower pot with the small end open and the other closed, while from the top springs a white heron's plume set into a socket, formed of a ruby as big as a hen's egg.

Chapter XV

ROYAL JEWELS NOT ALWAYS 'PRECIOUS'

NINETY thousand dollars for a necklace of amber! And bought at that price to sell again! Still, it had once belonged to the Empress Marie Louise of France and a guarantee to that effect went with it when Tiffany's of New York acquired it ten years ago. That alone would make such an ornament 'precious' even though amber is not now rated among the precious gems.

It was, once upon a time. But that was in the days of ancient Rome. Yet, who shall say that Rome over-rated it? After all, there is a golden glow about amber that re-acts beneficially upon its possessor in a way that not even the sheen of pearls can encompass.

Probably that was why the Romans deemed it to be a preventive of insanity, whether swallowed as a powder or worn round the neck as an amulet. Not that the French Empress Marie Louise is likely to have worn her amber necklace with that intent. But it is quite probable that the fame of amber among the Romans of old had something to do with her possession of such a jewel. Napoleon fancied himself as a Caesar.

There have been other royal ladies besides Napoleon's second wife, with a fondness for amber. One of them was that German-born Empress

I   153

Elizabeth of Russia whose husband was Tzar Nicholas I. She wore amber much as the Empress Marie Theresa of Austria wore pearls, that is, wound round and round her neck and then festooned about her bosom. Indeed, so much did this Russian Tzaritza love her amber beads that she was painted wearing them—six rows altogether, two of them so long that they still dangled below her waist after being caught up with a cameo brooch, as the miniature of her by Isabey in the Wallace Collection so captivatingly shows.

In view of her nationality before marriage, there may have been something more than personal delight behind that Russian empress's fancy for wearing amber. For though, ever since the Middle Ages, the port of Konigsberg in East Prussia on the Baltic has been the centre of the world's amber trade, ancient prestige may be all the better for being haloed with the publicity which the preferences of modern royalty can lend it. Germany, through Konigsberg, still handles most of the Baltic amber, though Riga the capital of neighbouring Latvia, rather specialises in amber trinkets, and presented a beautiful collection of amber jewellery to Queen Souriya of Afghanistan when she and King Amanullah were entertained there on their way to Moscow a few years ago.

Nor was that the first offering of amber to an Eastern Queen. Homer, in the *Odyssey*, tells of gold and amber chains being dangled before the eyes of the Queen of Syria and the ladies of her Court by a Phoenician trader, the while one of the palace women slipped away to his waiting vessel with the infant prince in her keeping.

Amber, the scientist says, is a fossil resin of extinct varieties of trees in forests submerged by the sea millions of years ago. Once, however, it was believed to be generated directly by the rays of the sun. But, according to Samland traditions, amber comes from the shattered submarine palace of Jurata the sea-queen which was destroyed by a thunderbolt because Jurata loved a mortal named Kastitis. Chained to a rock at the bottom of the sea, Kastitis can only voice his woes through raging storms and fierce tempests, and it is when these begin to subside that the time is good to go in search of what the amber fishermen call 'Baltic gold.'

Actually not a tenth of the amber that comes on the market is the harvest of the storms, else precious few would be the amber trinkets for woman's wear. Mining is the method most relied on, though even so only about twenty per cent of the amber thus secured from the 'blue earth' can be made into ornaments.

Her Imperial Majesty Marie Louise was not the first Empress of the French who deigned to wear jewels not always Precious. Her predecessor as Napoleon's consort, the luxury-loving Josephine, did so on occasions, and she was particularly fond of a set of cameos —diadem, necklace, earrings, brooch and coiffure combs—which had once been part of the Crown Jewels of the Two Sicilies.

Those royal cameos are still in existence, for though they were left behind by the last Empress of France—the Spanish-born Eugénie—when she fled to England in 1870, they escaped destruction in the burning of the Tuileries Palace by the Paris mob, and through purchase became the property of a distinguished Warwickshire family, the Lloyd-Bakers, in whose possession they now are.

What makes those cameos specially interesting to a student of royal trinkets is their setting: a narrow line of turquoise blue enamel between the lovely translucent golden shell and the plain band of beaten gold which rims them. That touch of blue would commend the cameos to Josephine no less than what the jewels stood for in Napoleon's career of conquest. She had a passion for colour and gave rein to it.

Maybe other emotions mingled with the pleasure Josephine had in those cameos. It could hardly be otherwise when her sister-in-law the Princess Pauline Borghese, as the wife of the head of a famous princely Italian family, had cameos to flaunt of an antiquity far greater than Josephine's. And did flaunt them. One historic occasion was a fancy ball at the Tuileries when Pauline represented 'Rome.' To quote Mr W. N. C. Carlton's *Pauline*:

Favorite sister to Napoleon, her "beautiful arms were encircled by golden bracelets set with the finest cameos. Her feet were shod with little sandals of purple silk with gold bands, and at each point where the band crossed the leg, a cameo was affixed." Moreover the ornament which held a small shield of golden scales to her breast above a tunic of gold embroidered muslin, "was the gem of the Borghese cameo collection, the one representing the Medusa dying. Those who remembered their classics were instantly reminded of the goddess Athene whose distinguishing attribute is the shield bearing the famous Gorgon's head. In her hand Pauline carried a light lance embossed with gold and precious stones."

Rather an envy-provoking vision, even to an empress! Especially as Josephine knew that Pauline possessed a superb cameo given her by the Pope when she paid her respects to him as a bride newly-arrived in Rome. No such Papal honour had come Josephine's way. But then, Pius the Seventh had not been pleased at being summoned to Paris to crown Napoleon, and Josephine's marriage had not been blessed by the church until the ceremony in the private chapel at the Tuileries late at night on the eve of the Coronation.

Much less often than royal consorts have royal favourites worn jewels that could not claim to be precious. For such ladies usually expected to feather their nests pretty well while under royal protection, and gifts of real gems were among their means of so doing. Hence the surprise at the Court of Louis XV when it was known that the King's mistress the Comtesse du Barry had accepted a pair of paste earrings. True they were very lovely earrings in a branching pendant design, and the stones might have been mistaken for diamonds and sapphires, though not by a jeweller.

Why such a powerful personage should wear imitation gems makes an interesting bit of jewel history. At that time the French national finances were in a bad way and the Minister of Finance, M. Silhouette, hit upon the idea of inviting wealthy folk to convert their jewels into coin for the benefit of the Treasury. But of course some striking example had to be set, and who better likely to be followed than the Du Barry? Thus came about the vogue for paste, strass and marcassite jewellery, which prevailed among the French *élégantes* in the middle of the eighteenth century.

That the vogue continued into the nineteenth century was due in a measure to the poverty which succeeded the French Revolution; at all events when the Duc de Berry married a Neapolitan princess Paris was so poor in diamonds that the wedding jewels offered the bride were mostly of strass.

Strass differed from paste in that it contained a higher percentage of lead, and marcassite differed from either by being a mined mineral and not a composition from an alchemist's crucible. Marcassite comes from Brazil and, according to the famous French jeweller Pouget the younger, who wrote a treatise on precious stones which was published in 1763, marcassite was called "pierre des Incas" because ornaments of this material had been found in the tombs of the Peruvians.

Before the close of the eighteenth century Paris had developed a passion for another substitute for precious stones—cut steel. Not that steel jewellery ever pretended to be other than it was, but the workmanship of it was so exquisite that it ousted real gems from favour for a time. And for that vogue Paris tapped an English source. It was Matthew Boulton of Birmingham who designed and made the first steel jewellery ever worn by civilized woman, and so originated a fashion which the famous French jeweller Dauffe developed along lines peculiarly French. For he called in the aid of the ivory-workers of Dieppe, with the result that bracelets of carved ivory medallions linked by filigree strands of finest cut steel, were soon causing Parisiennes to break the seventh commandment if they could not afford such ravishingly lovely trinkets.

Indeed both in England and France, steel cut and facetted for personal wear was so much sought after and became so expensive that only the very wealthy could possess it. Cut steel buttons were sold in Birmingham for as much as one hundred

and forty guineas a gross, so it was not much wonder that a dress embroidered in Paris with cut
steel beads cost the Princess Wurtemberg three
thousand francs.

Jet, too, has had its royal patrons. And on an
occasion of pomp and circumstance usually graced
only by the finest of precious stones. That was fifty
years ago when Queen Victoria appeared in a
diadem of jet at a Drawing-Room she held at
Buckingham Palace, and her daughters mingled
jet with their diamonds and pearls. The Royal
Family, being in mourning, the Queen, with her
charactersitic graciousness had yielded to a sug-
gestion that the time was fitting and opportune
for her to introduce the wearing of jet into Court
circles.

Whereupon prosperity came to Whitby with a
rush, and the jet-workers in that little Yorkshire
hill-town overlooking the North Sea, found themselves filling orders such as had never come Whitby way before in all the centuries of their craft's
existence. As every jeweller knows, the best jet in
the world is Whitby jet, and it needed only to have
been worn at the Court of St. James by the British
Sovereign herself, to set Republican France clam-
ouring for jet necklaces and crosses, jet brooches
and bracelets, and jet earrings, as well as jet flies
and jet insects of every kind with which to trim
hats and bonnets and caps. Even jet birds, jet
elephants, and jet tortoises in miniature, were

shipped from Whitby to Paris and were soon atop all the fashionable women's heads on both sides of the Channel.

Indeed, so great grew the demand for jet that jet-hewing on the Yorkshire cliffs became a lucrative occupation. Perhaps luck had something to do with the lucre, inasmuch as one man might strike a rich vein of jet within an hour of working, while another might labour for months without finding sufficient of the black rock to pay for his tools. And the better the jet the greater the noise in the getting of it, the hardest, and therefore the most desirable jet being usually in seams that had to be blasted with gunpowder.

There being no gunpowder in ancient times, the jet with which prehistoric woman decked herself was most likely picked up on the sea-shore. Very good jet, too, judging by the jet rings, and armlets, jet beads and buttons found in barrows of the bronze age. From the sea-shore also was probably garnered the jet used for rosary beads by the nuns and monks of Whitby Abbey.

According to Pliny the ancients called jet *gagates*, from Gagas in Lucia, where jet, or a similar substance, was originally found. And they used to say that jet mixed with the marrow of a stag would heal a serpent's bite. Such notions were scoffed at in Victorian England, though even to this day among the Basques of Northern Spain, jet is worn to ward off the Evil Eye. Especially from children, who, consequently, are oftener seen wearing jet beads than coral ones.

Spanish jet differs from Whitby jet in being less bright when mined and never taking on so fine a polish, no matter how much rouge may be used in the polishing process. The Spanish woman, however, prefers her jet thus, especially for the high comb upholding the lace mantilla she wears in church, a mantilla that must always be black and adjusted in a special way. And she has, or rather had, a royal example for her preference, as Queen Ena, her daughters the Infantas Beatrix and Cristina, and the ladies of the Spanish Court invariably wore jet combs with their black lace mantillas on occasions of public religious services in Madrid.

Many and various have been the royal trinkets immortalised in paint. But probably the rarest and strangest is the elephant's hair bracelet worn by Princess Marie Louise when she sat for her portrait a year or two ago to the American artist Mr Sneed Williams. That bangle had been given the Princess by an African chief when she was touring the Gold Coast, and as her picture showed she wore it just above the elbow on her left arm.

Chapter XVI
ROYAL ORDERS & JEWELLED DECORATIONS

AS IT is conferred by the British Sovereign at an Investiture, the badge of the Noble Order of the Garter, the oldest Order of Chivalry extant, is not jewelled. It is of dark blue velvet edged with gold and bearing the motto of the Order—"Honi soit qui mal y pense"—lettered in gold, the buckle and pendant being of chased gold. But it is permissable to embellish this historic leg-strap with precious stones—that worn by King Charles at his execution is said to have scintillated with four hundred brilliants. The last Emperor of Germany, William II, upon whom the honour was conferred when he was a lad of eighteen as a birth-day present from his maternal grandmother Queen Victoria, had his Star of the Order, which he still possesses, jewelled in rubies and diamonds. And Miss V. Sackville West, in her story of Knole, tells that the Garter which one of her ancestors, John Frederick Sackville, third Duke of Dorset, allowed an Italian dancer at the Paris Opera to wear as a hair bandeau, had the Garter's motto wrought in diamonds.

So has the Garter badge worn by Queen Mary when in Court dress. But it is hers by right as a Lady Companion of the Order, and it is worn as an armlet, not as a head-band. Rimmed in diamonds, also, is that other piece of the Order's insignia, the figure of St. George encountering the dragon, which her Majesty wears as a pendant to the Garter riband crossing her corsage from the left shoulder to the right hip. The collar of the Order, worn only by Knights, is composed of twelve "garters of chased gold, each centred by a red and white enamelled heraldic rose and alternating with knotted ropes of chased gold." From the collar hangs the George which, like the leg-strap, may be jewelled to the whim of the wearer. That pictured in a portrait of Henry Grey, Duke of Suffolk in the National Portrait Gallery, is enriched with a pearl cluster hanging from it like a pendant.

In the very early days of the Order of the Garter, gentlemen of every class were, under certain circumstances, eligible for the honour; and even a woman could be admitted a Lady Companion of the Order without having to be a reigning queen as has been the rule ever since the time of Henry VII. Testimony of this can be seen at Staunton Harcourt in Oxfordshire where the effigy on the tomb of a fifteenth century Lady Harcourt, has, so the learned antiquarians say, a sculptured representation of the badge of the Garter on the lady's left wrist.

Everyone knows the charming story of how the Garter badge originated: a splendid pageant at the Court of Edward III, the amazing and disconcerting mishap to the Countess of Salisbury, the King's tact in picking up the lady's dropped garter and checking the sniggers of the onlookers with his rebuke—"Honi soit qui mal y pense." Five hundred years or so later, at the Court of Queen Victoria, the garter which had become a symbol nearly wrecked another royal pageant, not by dropping off but by shifting indecorously awry on the leg of the blind Duke of Mecklenburg. Luckily the Duke of Connaught discovered and put straight the disarray, ere the lynx eyes of her Majesty had a chance of noting it.

Indeed, one way and another, the Order of the Garter has been the cause of considerable perturbation in royal circles. George III got agitated because, having made the Prince of Wales a Knight at three years old, he found he could not do the same by his many other sons if there were to be enough of such honours left for members of the nobility. So he had the Statutes of the Order altered to make the total number of knights 25 exclusive of the sons of the Sovereign. A century and a half later the Statutes were again altered, this time in circumstances more agitating still. The Garter had always been a decoration coveted by foreign royalties, but King Edward flatly refused to bestow it on the then Shah of Persia, because that monarch was not a Christian. True, a previous Shah had had the decoration and so had two Sultans of Turkey, but not at the hands of

King Edward. Eventually, however, for diplomatic reasons, his Britannic Majesty yielded to his Ministers' advice and had the Statutes of the Order amended to make non-Christians eligible; but he did not bestow the decoration personally on the Persian potentate. A Garter Mission was sent out to Teheran to hold an Investiture and give the Shah what he had so ardently longed for.

Which shows what a consequential part decorations play in exalted circles. Or did when crowned heads were more numerous in the world than they are to-day. Then it was a matter of pride with a royal personage on occasions of national and international importance like royal visits, royal weddings and royal anniversaries, to display the badges of the highest Orders of their own dominions, plus the decorations bestowed upon them by the rulers of other lands. Thus, when the Archduke Ferdinand of Austria came to England as the representative of his uncle the aged Emperor Francis Joseph at Queen Victoria's Diamond Jubilee celebrations, he brought with him the Order of the Golden Fleece, the highest decoration the Austrain Emperor had to bestow.

Like the badge of the Order of the Garter, that of the Golden Fleece in its original form lacks jewels, being a golden ram suspended by the middle from a firestone of gold. But the Austrian heir-apparent's decoration had been gemmed with the famous giant diamond known as the Star of Este, and that made it of colossal value. Yet no particular precautions were taken to guard it on the journey from Vienna to London. Along with a second royal badge gemmed with a ruby—an even more valuable treasure from the Este inheritance—the Golden Fleece badge was contained in a travelling bag carried by one of the Court officials in the Archduke's suite. No wonder Dr. Eisnemerger, the Archduke's physician, did not relish being given the bag to take care of when the royal party arrived at Dover. As he tells in his Memoirs; "With these treasure worth millions in my hands, I was pushed about and so shoved and jostled that I felt rather uncomfortable when I considered that one of the dozens of station thieves who were surely working near me at the moment, could capture such astonishingly rich spoils."

If not quite as ancient as the Order of the Garter, the Order of the Golden Fleece, which used to be in the power of both Austrian and Spanish monarchs to bestow, is like it in one respect; its origin is associated with a woman. For it was founded by Phillip II, Duke of Burgundy to commemorate his marriage with Princess Isabel of Portugal. Not that it was ever available for a woman as the Order of the Garter has been. Indeed its Statutes are much more rigid than those of the Garter, for no Protestant king may receive the honour without the consent of the Pope. Since 1429, the date of its foundation, the Order of the Golden Fleece

has been bestowed on nearly all the Catholic kings
and princes in Europe, the latest recipients being
the two youngest sons of the now exiled King Alfonso XIII of Spain, the Infantes Don Juan and
Don Gonzalo.

Queen Victoria set great store by Orders, and
after she became a widow usually wore six on the
corsage of her black silk gown whenever she held
a Drawing-room at Buckingham Palace. Two of
them were English—the Garter and the Victoria
and Albert; the third was known as the Saxe-
Coburg-Gotha Family Order, the remainder being Russian, Prussian, and Portuguese. The Russian Order, that of St. Catherine, was particularly
interesting because it had been founded by Tzar
Peter the Great to commemorate the affection and
heroism of his consort on the occasion of a battle
between the Russians and the Turks. At first men
were eligible for this decoration, but later it was
restricted to women and only those of the highest
rank, though they might be of any nationality.

Before Queen Victoria's time this Russian Order
had been conferred upon another English royal
lady, the eldest daughter of George III, H.R.H.
Charlotte Augusta, Princess Royal, who wore the
badge at her nuptials with the reigning Duke
(afterwards king) of Wurtemberg. It was a very
much jewelled badge, for not only did diamonds
rim the image of St. Catherine, but studded the
cross and the fleurs-de-lys which were part of the

device. In contrast, the other two foreign decorations which Queen Victoria meticulously displayed—the small gold cross enamelled in blue and black, of the Order of Louisa of Prussia, and the gold medallion bearing a representation of St. Isabella of Portugal—were comparatively plain.

Queen Mary does not make such a cult of the 'triumphal ornament' as did Queen Victoria, nevertheless she is entitled to wear the badges of four Orders, three that is, besides the Order of the Garter. And two of them are foreign, the French Legion of Honour and the Egyptian El Kemal, both, it is interesting to note, conferred upon her Majesty in the same year. But whereas the French Order is bestowed irrespective of sex, the Egyptian Order is for women only. 'El Kemal' means 'Perfection,' and King Fuad made pretty play on the word when decorating Queen Mary with the gold and enamel Star at Buckingham Palace in July 1927.

The Legion of Honour decoration which is a four-pointed star in silver, backed by a wreath half oak half laurel leaves, and inscribed with the words "Honneur et Patrie," has not always been available for women. Perhaps that is hardly to be wondered at, seeing that the Order was established by Napoleon I. But even Napoleon III would not bestow the honour on a woman, not even at the request of the Empress Eugénie, who thought it high time that Frenchwomen who had deserved well of their country should have the award. Particularly did the Empress wish the Legion of Honour for that great woman painter of animals, Rosa Bonheur. But no! the Emperor, or rather his Ministers, refused it, saying that as it had never hitherto been granted to a woman they protested against creating a 'precedent,' and refused to make an exception even to please the Empress.

However, they reckoned without the Imperial lady's determination and her ability to bide her time. And that time was not long in coming. Within twelve months or so of being snubbed by the Ministers of State the Empress had been proclaimed Regent during her husband's absence in Algeria, and so now being herself the head and fountain of all honour, she proceeded to do what the Emperor had not the courage to undertake. With her own hands she pinned the Cross of the Legion of Honour on the breast of Rosa Bonheur, and though the scene of the ceremony was the artist's studio and not the Tuilleries Palace, the Investiture was as valid as when M. Doumergue, as President of the French Republic, invested Queen Mary of England with the same decoration at Buckingham Palace seventy years later.

Queen Mary's fourth and newest decoration, which she wears as Dame Grand Cross of the Order of St. John of Jerusalem, is an eight-pointed cross of white enamel on gold with gold lions and unicorns in the principal angles. It is quite the most recent of all Order badges, for it represents a rank that was only created in 1927, though the Order itself was founded in Jerusalem as long ago as 1092, and was but eight years old when introduced into England. The day Queen Mary assumed that badge for the first time, the King invested five other royal ladies as Dames Grand Cross of the Order of St. John of Jerusalem—his daughter Princess Mary, his daughter-in-law the Duchess of York, his aunts the Duchess of Argyll and Princess Beatrice, and his niece Princess Arthur of Connaught.

Older than the Garter, older than the Golden Fleece, older even than the Order of St. John of Jerusalem, is the Order of the Golden Rose, a Papal honour, reserved for queens and princesses professing the Roman Catholic faith. The eleventh century is given as the date of its institution, though the first record of a Queen receiving the Golden Rose is in the fourteenth century, when Queen Johanna of Naples was so honoured by Pope Urban V. In by-gone times the Golden Rose was bestowed on Catholic kings as well as Catholic queens —our own Henry IV, Henry VIII and James III of Scotland all received it. So did other male royalties, for does not John Evelyn write in his diary under date March 25, 1645—"We went to the Vatican . . . The next day His Holiness was busied in blessing golden roses to be sent to several great Princes."

That, however, no longer obtains, and woman is singled out nowadays for this particular mark of the Pope's approval.

The Golden Rose is not a badge to be worn as a personal decoration on State occasions, but an object of art to be within the recipient's vision at all times. And that it may, it arrives complete with a vase, a two-handled affair of classic shape from which rises a straight and thorny stem of gold topped by a spray of foliage and roses expressed in filigree gold and precious stones. To give verisimilitude, the metal blooms are painted over in red, whiie cunningly concealed in the largest bloom is a receptacle for balm and musk placed there by the Pope when blessing the gift.

Royal ladies have sometimes been rather outspoken in the matter of Royal Orders when it has been a question of their subjects being honoured with such decorations by foreign monarchs. Queen Christina of Sweden would not permit the Prince Palatine to receive the Order of the Garter. Nor would Queen Elizabeth of England let two officers in her Navy keep the Collar of the Order of St. Michael conferred upon them by Henry II of France, but commanded them to send it back, her reason being that they had not first obtained her permission to accept the decoration. "I will not," she said, "have my sheep marked with a strange brand, nor suffer them to follow the pipe of a strange shepherd."

Chapter XVII
GIRDLES OF THE GREAT

WHEN future social historians come to delve into old newspaper files for data about twentieth
century fashions in jewellery, they will find awaiting them the fact that when Queen Mary's niece,
Lady May Cambridge, married a Commoner
(Captain Abel Smith) one of the gifts the bride
received from her parents Princess Alice and the
Earl of Athlone, was a diamond girdle. Moreover,
that the girdle was specially made from a special
design, and that that design in wax was shown
among the other wedding gifts at the reception
attended by her Majesty and the Prince of Wales.

In desiring a jewelled girdle, the Queen's niece
was following in a very old tradition. The girdle,
unjewelled, dates back to the time of the ancient
Medes and Persians, and has been an article of
both utility and ornament to every civilisation
since, be it Greek, Roman, Gallo-Roman or
Anglo-Saxon. But the earliest record of any royal
lady wearing a jewelled girdle is the figure, said to
be that of the fifth century Queen Clotilde, which
is represented on the door of the church of St.
German-des-Près, Paris.

That queen's girdle, however, does not suggest
the jewelled splendours which history credits to
another royal lady further East, the Empress
Theodora, consort of the Byzantine Emperor

Justinian, who ruled in Constantinople during the sixth century. Time and place had probably something to do with the difference, so, too, the Empress's early career as an actress and courtesan of renown. Nor was that all. There was her figure—a very graceful one by all accounts. That, most likely, was the real reason for the blaze of jewels with which she encircled her hips. How many jewelled girdles the Empress Theodora had to her name history does not tell, but when, nearly fourteen centuries later, the French actress, Sarah Bernhardt, impersonated her on the stage, eight jewelled girdles, varying in gems and design, were deemed necessary to the proper dressing of the part.

Back to France one must go for the sculptured record of another royal lady's girdle—the tomb at Le Mans, of Berengaria, the consort of Richard of England, though she never set foot in her husband's English dominions. Queen Berengaria's girdle differed from Queen Clotilde's and the Empress Theodora's in that attached to it was an aumonière or purse, proof and symbol of queenly charity to the poor and needy.

Not that the wife of Richard Coeur de Lion had as well filled an aumonière as she was entitled to, considering the continental dower she brought her husband. Richard spent too much on wars and crusades to leave anything but a very narrow margin for beneficence. And even at his death his widow could not get the annuity he had settled upon her—the revenues from the tin mines of Cornwall and Devon. Not even when she compounded for them with his successor, King John, at the rate of two thousand marks per annum to be paid half yearly. Pope Innocent took up the matter and threatened the kingly defaulter with an interdict if he did not pay the widowed queen her dues. But all to no purpose; and very thinly lined indeed would have been the aumonière hanging from the royal lady's girdle had not eventually the Templars become guarantors and agents for the payments.

John himself liked jewelled girdles, and those he wore were quite in keeping with his reputation for being the most extravagant prince in the world and the biggest fop in his dominions. At one Christmas festival his white damask tunic was girdled with garnets and sapphires, while the baldrick that crossed from the left shoulder to sustain his sword, was "set with diamonds and emeralds." Nor was John's son Henry III any less of a fop than his father, but he was more of a doting husband, and so his wife, Eleanor of Provence, fared well in the matter of jewels. To the tune of £30,000 at her coronation, it was said, her girdles alone being worth five thousand marks.

Indeed royalty in the Middle Ages had a passion for rich personal ornaments; even the unhappy Edward II who came to a ghastly end at the instigation of his infamous wife Isabella of France, fancied himself in jewelled girdles, one such ornament being "set with letters of pearls," the buckle pendant "enamelled with escutcheons of the Arms of England and others."

As for Isabella, her love for jewellery was notorious, and it did not abate with her banishment from Court in disgrace or the oncoming of old age. According to the Cottonian MSS in the British Museum Isabella spent on jewellery the equivalent of £16,000 in one currency during the years when she was virtually a prisoner first at Castle Rising and then at Hertford Castle, though being a widow her girdles were then less flambuoyant than of yore. One of the items in her personal expenses Accounts recorded in the Cottonian MSS. is for "a girdle of silk studded with silver, 20*s*.," a sum that would mean more than £10 nowadays.

By the time Catherine de Medici was queening it in France first as the wife and then the widow of the debased Henry II, and Elizabeth Tudor was reigning in England as queen in her own right, girdles had become a means of carrying many more useful articles than the aumonière or purse. Knives, scissors and keys hung from the housewife's girdle, while mirror-case, pomander, scent bottle and the indispensable fan, dangled from the girdle of the lady of fashion. Even books were hooked on to feminine girdles thenadays.

But they were mainly devotional books and

very beautiful to behold. One, that in her youth
Queen Elizabeth often wore at her girdle, was
of gold inlaid with red, green and black enamel
and decorated with a shell cameo, a very precious
cover for a very precious treasure—the last prayer
of her brother Edward VI in MSS. written on
vellum. History tells, too, of a "little boke of golde
enamuled, garnished and furnished with smale
diamonds and rubyes, with claspes, and all hanging at a chayne of golde," which was among the
New Year gifts offered to the Virgin Queen when
she had been reigning nearly a quarter of a century.

In all probability many of the girdles that had
encircled Elizabeth's waist came to be worn by the
wife of her successor James the Sixth of Scotland
and the First of England. For while he was 'pro-
gressing' from his northern kingdom to his newly
inherited southern territory, James wrote to the
English Council requesting that "as soon as Elizabeth's funeral was over, some of her ladies of all
degrees" should "journey to Berwick to meet
Queen Anne with such usual jewels and dresses
as were proper for her appearance in England."

Later, this 'Anna of Denmark' as she was before
her marriage, spent much money in jewelled girdles of her own choosing, but meanwhile, not having much siller, she was thankful to have the
reversion of any girdles that Queen Elizabeth had
left, though such was her spirit of contradiction

177

that she refused to appoint any of Elizabeth's ladies, except one, to offices in her bed-chamber.

Besides the girdles she inherited and the girdles
she bought, this, the first queen-consort of Britain,
had girdles that were gifts, notably one of "gold,
curiously enamelled," sent her by the Queen of
Spain in congratulation of King James's deliver-
ance from the Gunpowder Plot; and that the girdle might be suitably set off it was accompanied
by a dress and cap designed to wear with it. Just
listen to the official description of the complete
outfit—"A robe of murrey (mulberry) coloured
satin, braided all over with amber leather stamped
and sewed on, and outlined with gold lines, round
each device of leather were embroidered two gold
lines; each seam down the centre of the skirt also
embroidered to match. The forepart (front
breadth) was set with forty-eight tags, three
inches long, of beaten gold, hollow within and
filled with ambergris. Two carcanets (necklaces)
of ambergris. A murrey coloured velvet cap with
gold buttons curiously enamelled and a girdle suit-
able to the buttons. All which were presented in a
vessel of gold in the form of a bason."

Many celebrated ladies not queens, but often
more powerful than those who were, have been
wont to flaunt jewelled girdles in Court circles
Were expected to do so by such kings as Louis the
Fourteenth of France, whose passion for splendour
compelled all his Court, men as well as women, to

bedeck themselves with rich gems even if it meant mortgaging the family estates to do so. Louis XIV could not bear to look upon anything or anybody dull or drab—at least not until he fell under the spell of Madame de Maintenon. And this the Duchesse de Montespan well knew, hence her gold gaillote—the small boat used on the French rivers and canals—hung with scarlet damask and white banners, in which she went to meet Louis while she was doing a cure at the baths of Bourbon. Not that it made any difference to her supremacy in the long run. Louis, the 'Sun King,' eventually tired of this mistress as he had tired of others. Still, she took many jewels with her when she was driven from Court. Wore them, too, in her old age when she was a paying guest in a convent, though, to quote Miss Maud Cruttwell "her garters, bracelets and girdles encrusted with jewels on the outside, were lined with iron points."

That seems to have been the moment in the girdle's career when its partial eclipse began. Louis the Fourteenth was by that time being considerably influenced by "the eminent refrigerator" as Robida calls Madame de Maintenon, and she never drew attention to her hips by encircling them with gems. Fashion, however, really deposed the girdle when it brought in the stiff pointed bodice and wide panniered skirts which characterised women's dress in the eighteenth century. So the girdle never got any *réclame* from either

Madame de Pompadour or Madame du Barry, nor from Queen Marie Antoinette. It had to wait for the Empress Josephine to restore its prestige. Which she did by wearing it at her coronation.

But not outlining her hips. The pseudo-classical high-waisted dresses this French Empress made the rage needed the girdle to emphasise the bosom. And so it does very effectively in David's grandiose painting of the Coronation of Napoleon and Josephine in Notre-Dame, exhibited in the Louvre. The jewelled girdles of Napoleon's sisters who were carrying Josephine's train can be seen set with cameos, and Josephine's girdle probably was also, though it is obscured in the picture by her horizontally extended, half-raised arms, and the velvet manteau de Cour she wears over her white silk dress embroidered with gold bees. For the first Empress of the French had at this time a consuming passion for cameos, and had badgered Napoleon into letting her have the antique cameos and intaglios from the State collection in the Royal Library set for her personal wear.

Only thus could she keep ahead of her sister-in-law the Princess Pauline Borghese, who had the Borghese heirlooms, the world famous collection of cameos, to go at. In Lefêvre's portrait of her which hangs at Versailles, the Princess Pauline is depicted wearing a high comb, bandeau, earrings and girdle, all decorated with cameos.

Where Josephine could always score over Pauline was in her right as Empress to decorate her girdle with the Imperial gold bees. And this she did very ingeniously on one occasion when she wanted to display some pear-shaped emeralds in an unusual manner. Each of these gems was fastened pendant-wise to a mitred end of a satin tab encrusted with gold bees, and the tabs hung from a narrow band of massed seed pearls encircling her high-waisted satin gown. With this uncommon girdle the Empress wore a tiara, necklace and long earrings of emeralds and pearls, and so liked herself in the ensemble that she had the artist Gerard paint her thus attired, a picture which now hangs at Malmaison. Pauline's counterblast to this was the dazzling girdle of diamonds and mock emeralds which one of her biographers puts down as costing thirteen thousand francs and looking worth a million.

Much less of a sensation was made by the girdles of Napoleon's second wife the Austrian-born Marie Louise. For one thing she never attempted to set the fashions as Josephine had done, nor was she as extravagant as Josephine. Then, too, as the mother of the little King of Rome, she had all the adulation, public and private, that her heart desired. Still, there are Napoleon's letters to tell that on his advice she took all her personal treasure with her when she quitted France at the time of his abdication, and there is her own Last Will and Testament to prove that there was at least one jewelled girdle among that treasure. For, when she died of cholera thirty-four years later, it was found that she had bequeathed to an English friend, Lady Burgersh, a girdle set with Imperial bees in pearls and coral, a jewel now in the possessiou of Lady Burgersh's granddaughter, Miss Rachel Weigall.

Lady May Cambridge, whose diamond girdle gave the keynote to this chapter, is not the only royal lady to receive a jewelled girdle as a wedding gift. Just fifty years earlier — in May, 1881 — Princess Stephanie of Belgium, on her marriage with the Crown Prince Rudolph of Austria, had been presented by the Hungarian city of Pesth with a girdle formed of gold chains held together by medallions of rubies and brilliants. Apart from its intrinsic worth that jewelled girdle was an enviable possession because it was a copy of one that had been made for a renowned sixteenth century royal lady—Queen Isabella Zapolyi of Hungary.

Chapter XVIII
NECKLACES OF FAME AND FASCINATION

WHAT is probably the oldest existing jewelled necklace that has been worn by a queen both in England and Scotland, is neither a royal nor a State possession. It belongs, as a family relic, to the Premier peer of the Realm, his grace the Duke of Norfolk, Hereditary Earl Marshal of England. In the sixteenth century it clasped the milk-white throat of Mary Queen of Scots, and was one of the jewels she brought with her when she escaped from Loch Leven castle and came south of the Tweed in the hope of finding protection under the wing of her cousin Queen Elizabeth of England.

"Designed to sit closely yet lightly on a slender neck, it is composed apparently of half pearls set in a kind of filigree and connected by gold links of minutely exquisite handiwork," is how this royal necklace was described by a guest at the marriage of the present Duke of Norfolk's father to his first wife Lady Flora Hastings. Nearly two centuries had elapsed since, in 1683, a Howard holding the dukedom had married, and this royal and priceless relic was the premier gift of the nineteenth century duke to his bride. Actually, in point of splendour, it was eclipsed by the diamond necklace which was one of the bridegroom's other gifts, but those 'half pearls' stirred the imagination as no mere dazzling gems, however superb, could do. For tradition says this pearl necklace was one of the love tokens Mary Stuart sent to Howard, fourth Duke of Norfolk, whom she pledged herself to marry although they had never seen each other. Perhaps that was why he disavowed her when Elizabeth clapped him into the Tower of London. Mary Stuart's pearl necklace now abides at Arundel Castle in Sussex, though there was a time when its spiritual home would have seemed to be more fittingly at Sheffield in South Yorkshire. For it was at Manor Castle, Sheffield, within bowshot of where the late Duke of Norfolk had a residence up to his death in 1917, that the ill-fated queen was a prisoner when she heard the news of *her* Duke of Norfolk's execution, and thereupon "did not leave her chamber for a week."

If none of Queen Elizabeth's necklaces have come down to posterity, there is plenty of documentary and pictorial evidence that they were very gorgeous ones. New Year gifts many of them were, offerings from would-be suitors or Courtiers who wished to stand high in the royal lady's favour. When she had been reigning twenty-three years the Earl of Leicester gave her a "chaine of gold made like a pair of beads containing eight long pieces garnished with small diamonds and four score and one small pieces garnished with like diamonds." Foreign potentates also helped to fill 'Gloriana's' jewel casket. It is told that the mother of the Sultan Amurath III of Turkey, hearing of the English queen's passion for pearls, sent her a pearl and ruby necklace, companioning it by a rich gown and several handkerchiefs of silk embroidered with gold.

But the pearl necklaces Elizabeth wears in such profusion in many of her portraits were mainly composed of the pearls that had belonged to Mary Queen of Scots and bought by her, Elizabeth, at a bargain price. How early this passion for pearls developed is revealed by that portrait of Elizabeth at Windsor taken at the age of thirteen or fourteen. For the picture depicts her wearing a head-dress rimmed with pearls, a jewelled corsage ornament fringed with three drop pearls, and a pearl pendant attached to the string of pearls that is twisted twice round her neck.

If some historians are to be believed, the fashion for wearing necklaces of precious stones as we know them to-day, originated with Agnes Sorel the mistress of the fifteenth century French King Charles VII. Be that as it may, necklaces before her time were not the dazzling adornments they became after it, at least not in western Europe and in Britain. One of the best pictured presentations of a jewelled necklace worn by a royal personage of that period outside France, is the portrait of Queen Margaret wife of James III of Scotland,

n 185

which hangs at Holyrood. The necklace depicted
is a double row of pearls connected by oval jewelled medallions and hung with a ruby-gemmed
pendant, but whether it actually belonged to the
Queen seems open to doubt. For a precisely similar necklace adorns an Italian lady in a painting by
the same artist—the Flammand, Van der Goes,—
which hangs in the Uffizi Gallery at Florence!

Pearls! how persistently they crop up in the history of royal Courts! But they were not always
real. 'Monsieur' the only brother of Louis XIV of
France and about the biggest fop and the biggest
glutton at Versailles, left debts at his death to the
tune of seven and a half million francs, with the
result that 'Madame' his widow, had to sell all her
jewels even to the pearls she had been in the habit
of wearing. Not that thereafter she went bare-
necked and unadorned. "Since the late Monsieur's
death" (she wrote to a friend,) "I have worn only
false pearls, but they are so exactly like the ones I
had before that everyone thinks them the same. I
was once with the Queen of England at St. Ger-
main, and, in coughing, the pearls broke from my
neck. The Queen threw herself on the ground to
search for the pearls. I helped her up and said:
'Ah, Madame, your Majesty must not take this
trouble. I am very munificent, I will leave my
pearls to your people.' The Queen looked at me
and said, 'God pardon me, from this discourse I
almost fear they are false.' I answered, 'Madame,

186

you have said it.' The Queen had never noticed it, nor anyone else."

That century—the eighteenth—saw a bigger hullaballoo about a necklace at the French Court —this one of diamonds—real gems—ordered by Louis XV for his mistress Madame du Barry, and, left on the jeweller's hands, offered to and refused by Queen Marie Antoinette wife of Louis XVI, only to involve her in a law suit that brought disgrace and odium on her already unpopular personality. A fraction of that historic necklace was on view in London a little time ago, and certainly the size of the stones looked 'royal' enough. But one had to go home and read Carlyle's quaint yet vivid description of it, and study an old print that had been a frontispiece to *L'Affaire du Collier*, printed in Paris in 1785, to get an idea of what the famous necklace had looked like in its entirety nearly a century and a half ago, before it was surreptitiously despatched to London to be broken up. Wrote Carlyle—"A row of seventeen glorious diamonds, as large almost as filberts, encircle, not too tightly, the neck, a first time. Looser, gracefully fastened thrice to these, a three-wreathed festoon and pendants enough (simple pear-shaped multiple star-shaped or clustering amorphous) encircle it, enwreath it, a second time. Loosest of all, softly flowing round from behind, in priceless catenary, rush down two broad threefold rows; seem to knot themselves, round a very Queen of

Diamonds, on the bosom; then rush on, again separated, as if there were length in plenty; the very tassels of them were a fortune for some men. And now lastly, two other inexpressible threefold rows, also with their tassels, will, when the Necklace is on and clasped, unite themselves behind in a doubly inexpressible *sixfold* row; and so stream down, together or asunder, over the hind-neck— we may fancy, like lambent Zodiacal or Aurora-Borealis fire."

Josephine, the next Empress of the French, never wore her necklaces like that. But then, fashions changed radically after the Revolution and during the First Republic, and when Napoleon restored the Monarchy his Empress had a mind to wear her jewels differently from her predecessors on the throne, though she was similar in her extravagant liking for such gewgaws.

In previous chapters I have told of Josephine's ruby necklace, her emerald and pearl necklace, her parure of cameos. Perhaps more famed and fascinating than even those, was another necklace, now in the possession of the Hon. Mrs Lionel Cust composed of twelve antique sardonyxes engraved with classical subjects and surrounded with brilliants, the sardonyxes linked together by gold filigree gemmed with pearls. Another relic of Josephine's onetime passion for antique jewels is treasured at the Ashmolean Museum, Oxford, and is a bullae, that is a spherical pendant of gold such as Roman women used to wear attached to their necklaces. It was found at Herculaneum and was presented by the Court of Naples to Napoleon's first wife.

Historians have had much less to say about the necklaces of Napoleon's second wife, the Empress Marie Louise. Probably because she ceased to be of importance in European politics when she came under the domination of General Niepperg, whom Austrian intrigue deliberately placed in command of her household in order to alienate her affections from Napoleon, and so prevent her joining him on the Island of Elba. But as long as the picture endures Gerard's portrait of her with the little King of Rome, will tell the world of the magnificent diamond and pearl necklace Napoleon gave her on the birth of their son, a love-gift that remained in the Austrian Imperial family until 1930 and then became the subject of litigation in the American law courts. Still, when all is said about Napoleon's two Empresses and their jewels, about the Princess Pauline his favourite sister and her passion for costly trinkets, it remains with his step-daughter Hortense, Queen of Holland, to achieve the most romantic gesture with gems that shine. For when the Emperor's fortunes were at the lowest ebb and he was leaving Malmaison for the last time, she offered him her diamond necklace, and herself stitched it into his waistcoat for security. And this gift-necklace he kept unto the end, bequeathing it to his valet Marchand when he lay dying at St. Helena.

It is recorded that when Napoleon III was deposed from the throne of France, all the money he had in the world was £60,000. Luckily his wife, the Empress Eugénie, had been able to bring most of her big collection of valuable jewels away with her, and she possessed Spanish properties besides. So, by gradually selling her jewels and wisely investing the proceeds, she was able to live in comfort the forty-three years she survived the Emperor. According to unpublished documents in the Palacio de Liria the Madrid residence of the Duke of Alba, quoted by Mr Robert Sencourt in his *Life of the Empress Eugénie*, the chief purchaser of the exiled French Empress's jewels was Rothschild. But there were other bidders and buyers at Christie's in 1872 when 114 'lots' of this royal lady's jewels were put up for auction. That was the occasion when one of her necklaces, a string of "forty-one large pearls of the highest quality, with cluster brilliant snap" was acquired by the Marquis of Bristol for £2,400. The Empress's famous diamond necklace, which scintillated on the mauve brocade coat of the twenty-years-old Maharajah of Patiala at the Delhi Durbar in 1911, was bought privately, but the sum paid for it by the grandfather of the present Maharajah did not leak out. It is known, however, that the Sanci diamond, another jewel out of

France, which on State occasions the Maharajah wears as a pendant to the by-gone empress's necklace, was valued at three lakhs of rupees.

In the Russian Imperial Treasure of jewels is a diamond necklace known as 'Le Collier d'esclave,' which contains thirty-six large diamonds, fifteen of them pear-shaped and pendant to the twenty-one round gems. They are Indian stones, and it was their lovely colour, some bluish, some of pink water, that made the necklace a favourite ornament with the Tzaritza Maria-Feodorovna, mother of the last Tzar. Favourite that is, among the State jewels, her first favourite was the great triple diamond necklace which was a gift from her husband Alexander II. Indeed the one necklace set off the other amazingly, and so were often worn together even when she became Dowager Empress, since her son's wife the Empress-consort preferred pearls round her own neck and rarely raided the Crown diamonds for her adorning. And when the collier d'esclave and the triple diamond necklet were worn together at such functions as the service in the chapel of the Winter Palace on the day of the ceremonial Blessing of the Waters of the Neva by the Emperor, the Imperial lady's head-dress would be the national Kakoshnik in silver blazing with diamonds, and her gown all silver brocade hemmed with sable. For so tradition decreed.

Once upon a time, and that not so very long ago

—to be exact it was in the year 1683—a royal necklace was advertised as the chief prize in a lottery. It had belonged to Prince Rupert a nephew of Charles I, who had made him Governor of Windsor, and the jewel was in the market owing to the Prince's death. Indeed so were all his jewels, and this lottery "was planned to dispose of them at a moderate value" as the advertisement had it. The necklace was a pearl one, and valued at eight thousand pounds, which was more than a third of the rest of the jewels put together, the whole lot having been appraised by a firm of jewellers at £20,000 all told. To encourage 'adventurers' to take tickets, King James II gave his patronage to the lottery and even promised to be present "to read the Prizes and mix them with the Blanks." But seemingly all to no purpose, for the newspapers of the period were silent as to whether the lottery came off, and nothing further was publicly heard of Prince Rupert's pearl necklace.

Chapter XIX
BEAUTEOUS BOXES

IF, as social historians of the eighteenth century are apt to say, that period was truly the age of boxes, surely the nineteenth and twentieth centuries can claim to be equally distinguished for royal collectors of such trifles. The Empress Eugénie of France made a hobby of collecting jewelled patch-boxes, sweetmeat-boxes and snuff-boxes; and a very profitable hobby it turned out to be, when, exiled in England, she decided to convert her treasures into cash and had them sold at Christie's in 1872.

Now it is Queen Mary, consort of King George V of England and Emperor of India, whose flair for beauteous boxes agitates the antique dealers. And perhaps to greater purpose. For Queen Mary does not hoard the choice things she buys; many go to enrich public museums and others are photographed for publication in art magazines. A year or two ago her Majesty presented to the Royal United Services Institution Museum in Whitehall, a tortoiseshell and silver snuff-box that had been made to commemorate the Battle of Trafalgar.

Patches came before snuff in the history of civilisation. For senators and others wore them in the decadent days of the ancient Roman Empire. So when Court ladies in the seventeeth century in

England and France took to 'patching' their faces, they were but reviving an old fashion, though the revival certainly far outdid the original mode. Six or seven patches were quite usual on a woman's face then, and they were of all shapes— moons and stars, squares and crescents and even a coach and horses! They were named, too: 'Roguish,' 'Gallant,' 'Kissing,' 'Majestic,' 'Murderous,' 'Playful,' according to the particular position they occupied on the feminine countenance.

Besides that, patches could have a political significance. In the reign of Queen Anne English ladies of consequence with Whig sympathies patched on the right cheek, while Tory ladies patched on the left. And as no patch could be guaranteed to stay put the livelong day, and a woman might need to change her patches with her moods when away from her dressing-table, there had to be boxes for them of a size a woman could carry about with her, and of a beauty that would not mar the grace and fantasy of her toilette. One patch-box made for a lady of fashion at the Court of Louis XIV was shaped like a vase and made of agate delicately mounted with gold, while on the lid was a small enamelled figure seated in a circlet of diamonds. When that patch-box changed hands at Christie's some years ago it fetched £2,150.

A great price, that, and most likely so because there are few seventeenth century patch-boxes now in existence, either publicly or privately own-

ed. But probably more people thrilled to the romance of an eighteenth century patch-box of tortoiseshell mounted in gold, that was sold in London last year when the effects of Lucy, Countess
of Egmont, came under the hammer at her house
in Eaton Square. For, inside the lid of that patch-
box was the miniature of a by-gone Countess, the
adored wife of the second Earl of Egmont who
married her when she was seventeen, in 1732.
After the birth of their seventh child the Earl was
told that his wife could not live long. So he sat by
her bedside and enshrined her memory in the
miniature.

The French King Louis the Fourteenth's mor-
ganatic wife Madame de Maintenon disdained
patches and patch-boxes, though in her youth,
when tending her aunt's turkeys, she had worn a
mask to protect her face from the sun. Snuff and
snuff-boxes were also abhorrent to her; indeed she
thought snuff-taking a disgusting habit and com-
plained bitterly of the "noses of the Court ladies
brown with snuff." She was, however, fond of
sweets, and one of the last gifts she received from
Louis was a bonbonnière or sweetmeat-box. It
was one of the things Louis had found in his pock-
ets when, with her help, he had searched through
his clothes as he lay ill in bed of the malady from
which he died. It was a "plain round box of tortoiseshell," says one of Madame de Maintenon's
biographers. One can hardly imagine this king,

"the Sun King," in his younger days, offering "plain tortoiseshell" to, say, Madame de Montespan—the tortoiseshell would have had to be gold-mounted at least, if not bejewelled as well, to satisfy that rapacious lady. Still, tortoiseshell has always enjoyed royal favour. Philip of Spain, a grandson of Louis XIV of France gave his bride a bonbonnière of tortoiseshell elaborately mounted in gold with an interlaced cypher and crown on the lid, and a miniature of himself inside.

But tortoiseshell did not appeal to the fair and frail ladies who made gay the life and Court of Louis the Fifteenth. It was much too sombre-looking a substance for their roguish frivolity. They preferred gold enlivened with coloured and translucent enamels, or gold enframing adaptations of paintings of genre scenes. Some of the most fascinating sweetmeat-boxes of the Louis Quinze period that have been preserved for posterity show on the lids pictures in miniature obviously inspired by the Fêtes Galantes of Fragonard, the pastoral idylls of Boucher, and subjects in the style of Teniers and other Dutch artists. There was, too, for a time, a rage for classical subjects as decorative motifs on sweetmeat-boxes, so that ladies of fashion went about carrying painted representations of the gods and goddesses of Roman mythology in their handbags. One such bonbonnière of rock crystal and gold, now treasured at Hertford House, London, has on the lid a profile

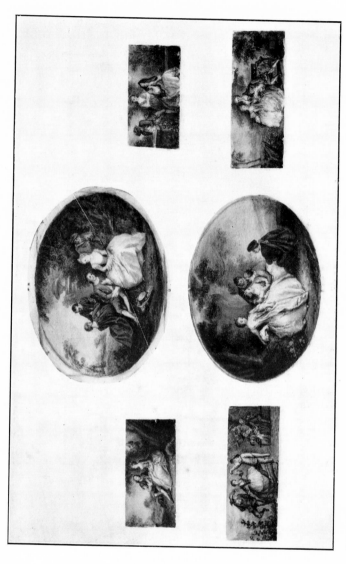

Examples of patch boxes, sweetmeat boxes and snuff boxes once belonging to the Empress Eugenie of France, who was a great collector of such objets d'Art. The lids of these beauteous boxes are embellished with gouache paintings in the style of Fragonard and Boucher.

By permission of the Trustees of the Wallace Collection.

To face page 196.]

head and bust of Bellona, the Goddess of War, a theme that may or may not have been intended as a satire on the scandal of Metz. That scandal, due to the effrontery of the King's mistress Madame de Chateauroux in joining Louis while he was with his Army and when the Queen had been left behind at Versailles, gave rise to a popular ditty, maliciously hummed by the troops on march:

"Belle Chateauroux, je deviendrai fou,
    Si je ne vous baise.

Most sweetmeat-boxes of eighteenth century craftsmanship were either oblong, oval or round, and about three inches in length. Some creators of such elegant trifles did, however, occasionally dare to be fantastic, and so it comes about that in the Wallace Collection, is a bonbonnière made by the famous Jean Ducrollay, which has a top shaped like a shell and is decorated with peacock feathers enamelled in colours on white. Even more fantastic, and probably dating from about the time when Madame de Pompadour held sway at Versailles, is one of gold in the form of a bath, decorated inside the lid with a relief of Neptune commanding the waves.

So much for the bonbonnière. But whereas Fashion decreed its vogue on both sides of the Channel, custom, and a very ancient one at that, accounted for a similar elegant trifle, the *dragée* box peculiar to France. A *dragée* box, as its name implies, is intended to hold those sugared almonds which, from time immemorial, have always made their appearance at christenings in well-to-do French families, and which must be duly despatched to any relative or important family friend unable to 'assist' at the festival. *Dragées* also used to be the traditional sweetmeat at French weddings; and when the eldest daughter of Louis XV married the King of Spain, the city of Paris gave her, among other things, twelve dozen boxes of sugared almonds—small painted boxes which, when emptied of their toothsome contents, could be used for holding odds and ends on the royal lady's toilet-table. A feature of *dragée* boxes was that they nearly always had glass lids, and such lids were painted with scenes and figures in wonderful colours. One *dragée* box shown in an interesting collection of these trifles in London a few years ago, was, however, a departure from the usual, in that its lid bore a model, executed in mother-of-pearl and gold, of Jeanne d'Arc's house at Domrémy.

When it comes to eighteenth century snuff-boxes, much the same tale of beauty and brilliance can be told. For thenadays man, no less than woman, liked the accessories of his costume to be rich and rare, and he spent much thought and money to get them so. There is in existence an oval-shaped gold Louis Quinze snuff-box from the Em-

Patch, sweetmeat and snuff boxes in gold, mother of pearl, translucent enamels and Chinese lacquer, mostly seventeenth and eighteenth century work. The centre box in the top row is shaped like a bath.

By permission of the Trustees of the Wallace Collection.

To face page 198.]

press Eugénie's collection that has, framed in the lid, sides and bottom, coloured enamels portraying a lion hunt and other oriental subjects, while along the rim is an interlaced ribbon of diamonds.

Not that the Empress collected only what was French-made. She specialised rather in period than in place. Of German origin was one of her eighteenth century snuff-boxes, and very remarkable it was, being of cornelian mounted in gold, and having on the lid, wrought in cornelian, a cameo relief of Leda and the Swan. Neuber of Dresden had made it at a time when French jeweller-craftsmen were favouring that other quartz, onyx, and even more so, Sèvres porcelain and engine-turned enamel, as the basis of snuff-boxes. King Stanilaus of Poland, whose daughter Marie Leczinska became Queen-consort of Louis XV of France, used a Paris-made snuff-box of dark blue enamel overlaid with arabesques of gold, and inset on the lid with a medallion of Venus and Cupid done in coloured enamels.

Royal portraits have adorned both patch-boxes and snuff-boxes, but not always have portrait and box been contemporary in workmanship. You can see at Hertford House, London, a gold patch-box of English make thought by the authorities there to have been made in Sheffield in the early nineteenth century, that has inset three miniatures, one of Louis XIV, the second of his mistress Louise Duchesse de Vallière, and the third of a youthful

Cardinal long said to be Cardinal Fleury. The
minature of the King, showing him wearing the
lace jabot which he popularised in France for
national industry's sake, has been indentified by a
signature on the back as the work of Henri Toutin,
one of a family of enamellers from Blois; moreover
it must have been executed in the early seventies
of the seventeenth century, probably 'after' a portrait by Mignaud. Yet here it is adorning a box
that is thought to have been made in the hill-girt
town of Sheffield in South Yorkshire, when George
the Third was King.

Louis XIV was not always portrayed in everyday garb. There are snuff-boxes extant bearing
miniatures depicting him clad in armour, in Court
dress, and arrayed as one or other of the classical
characters he was fond of impersonating in the
amateur theatricals which enlivened the Court at
Versailles during the early part of his reign. In the
Empress Eugénie's collection was a gold snuff-
box adorned with a picture said to represent Louis
and Madame de Montespan as the lovers in Tasso's
epic *Rinaldo*. Of later date, and once belonging to
Prince Demidoff, is a snuff-box of gold and translucent blue enamel, that bears on the cover, set in
diamonds, a miniature of the Duchesse de Bour-
gogne, consort of the son of the Grand Dauphin
and grandson of Louis XIV.

Even a whole Court has enlivened a snuff-box
lid. For one of the famous Blarenberghe brothers

PATCH, SWEETMEAT, AND SNUFF BOXES. Side views of the examples shown on a previous page. By permission of the Trustees of the Wallace Collection.

To face page 200.]

did a gouache miniature of Louis Seize and Marie Antoinette surrounded by their entourage in the sylvan precincts of an imposing chateau, and that painting was fitted into the cover of an oval-shaped snuff-box of gold wrought and chased and coloured in two tints. Such a box is alluringly beautiful. And how differently it stirs the imagination from that other of our national possessions, the snuff-box given to the Hon. Mrs Damer by Napoleon Bonaparte, and bearing his portrait blatantly rimmed with big diamonds.

Some of the most beauteous boxes ever carried about by by-gone men and women of fashion, were designed primarily in the interests of hygiene and date from the days when street-sanitation was non-existent and palaces stank in their State apartments hardly less than in the lacqueys' quarters. Vinaigrettes, such boxes were called, and that because they contained, behind a hinged grille, the tiny piece of sponge soaked in aromatic vinegar, then believed to be the best antidote against evil smells and noxious vapours.

Silver was the usual material for the making of vinaigrettes, and the fashion was to have it engraved with the owner's name or initials, plus, perhaps some pretty sentiment like "Forget-me-not." Another fashion favoured vinaigrettes embossed with views of castles and cathedrals, Windsor and Warwick being the castles preferred.

Exclusive folk, however, would have their silver gilt, and then the vinaigrette would often be given a lid of agate. Or, when gold was the chosen metal, its fashionable complement might be topaz, step-cut to bring out the full beauty of the stone; or cornelian engraved with figures of classic fame. And how tiny the vinaigrettes were: never more than two inches by one and a half inches, and sometimes not as much as that. One lovely vinaigrette now preserved in London at the Victoria and Albert Museum, is made out of two emeralds seven eighths of an inch in height and seven eighths of an inch across. No wonder it realised one hundred and forty five guineas when it was sold by auction in 1886 and that one bidder described it as "Titania's toy."

BIBLIOGRAPHY

BACKHOUSE, E., & J. O. P. BLAND. Annals
and Memories of Peking.

BOWEN, MARJORIE. The Third Mary Stuart.

CONWAY, SIR MARTIN. Art Treasures of
Soviet Russia.

COOK, E. THORNTON. Royal Marys.

CRUTTWELL, MAUD. Madame de Maintenon.

DAGGETT, MABEL POTTER. Marie of
Roumania.

ERCOLE, LUCIENNE. Gay Court Life:
France in the 18th Century.

EVANS, JOAN. Magical Jewels.

FORVAL, CLAUDE. Private Life of Cleopatra.

HENDERSON, E. F. A Lady of the Old
Régime.

JONES, WILLIAM. Crowns and Coronations.

JONES, WILLIAM. Finger Ring Lore.

JONES, WILLIAM. History and Mystery of
Precious Stones.

LICHTERVELDE, COMTE LOUIS DE.
Leopold of the Belgians.

LING, PRINCESS DER. Old Buddha.

MIDDLETON, J. H. Engraved Gems of Classical Times.

ODDIE, E. M. Marie Louise.

PAVITT, W. T. & K. The Book of Talismans and
Precious Stones.

RADZIWILL, PRINCESS CATHERINE. Nicholas II the last of the Tzars.

RICHARDSON, NORVAL. Mother of Kings.

SENCOURT, ROBERT. Life of the Empress Eugénie.

SMITH, CLIFFORD. Jewellery.

STOPFORD, FRANCIS. Romance of the Jewel.

STRICKLAND, AGNES. Queens of England.

Investigations & Studies in Jade (The Bishop Collection, Metropolitan Museum of Art, New York, U.S.A.)

The Gemmologist.

Encylopædia Britannica.

INDEX